As Simple As Breathing
On Yoga, Writing, and Life

Leah Carey

Illustrations by
Arthur G. Scholz

Copyright © 2015 Leah Carey

All rights reserved. This book may not be reproduced in whole
or in part, stored in a retrieval system, or transmitted in any form
or by any means—electronic, mechanical, or other—without
written permission from the publisher, except by a reviewer,
who may quote brief passages in a review.

ISBN: 0986280305
ISBN-13: 978-0-9862803-0-6

To Carl,
who always believed I would find the words.

CONTENTS

Preface	ix
On Clarity	1
On Body and Mind	9
On Hiding	17
On Self-Doubt	25
On Intention	31
On Conquering Fear	37
On Self-Confidence	43
On Parenting	47
On Friendship	53
On Choices	61
On Loss and Grief	67
On Fairness	75
On Equality	83
On Spirituality	93
On Love	101
On Writing	107
On Vulnerability	113
Acknowledgements	119
About The Author	121

PREFACE
VICTORIUS BREATH, UJAYI PRANAYAMA

Whenever you practice yoga, it is essential to focus first on your breath practice, your pranayama. Inhale deeply through your nose to fill your belly and rib cage. Exhale slowly through your nose so the air goes out at the same rate as it came in. Concentrate on breathing continuously in this simple and powerful way to clear your mind and warm your body. The rhythmic sound of air passing through you is like the sound of the ocean waves as they arrive on the shore. As each wave of breath comes in, there is a pause. As each wave of breath goes out, there is a pause. In the space between these breaths you begin to connect with your limitless potential.

Each of us has the opportunity to share our gifts with the world. This is a tricky proposition, though. It takes time to understand one's gifts and time to understand the world. It is no surprise that many of us wake up at mid-life and see things differently. After all the doing and being for others in our small circles of existence we recognize that we have more and are more. Maybe we always sensed this, but the fog has finally cleared and we can see it. It is hard to look away.

For me, receiving these messages was a painful experience. I was approaching 50 and confronted with the results of my non-doing and non-being. I felt I had run away from my essential, creative self and I had done this in complicated ways. The messages had been arriving at a fast and furious pace. In my role as an executive and organizational coach, I attended a leadership seminar in May 2010 that was focused on better understanding who we each were as leaders so that we could better coach others. An intensive profile was created based on feedback from bosses, peers, and those we managed. The night before receiving the feedback, I hardly slept; I was anxious to know how others saw me. When I finally opened my packet, I was surprised. The ratings and comments were positive, with a twist. The message was "you're not playing as big as you could, you're not using all of your potential, you're not being courageously authentic. You're hiding your light, and you already know it." I heard this from the seminar leaders and participants over and over again. I told close friends and they said, "yes, obviously!" It was painful to feel that I had wasted time. It was liberating to have been given permission—to give myself permission—to pursue all the wild and wonderful ideas that regularly appeared in my consciousness.

For a while, I dabbled in the world of socially-conscious business. It was exciting to be an entrepreneur, but ultimately a distraction from who I am and my purpose. Instead of bringing me closer to that answer, it felt like I was drifting further from it. After a year, I went back to leadership consulting—work that does feel like more of a calling—but I still felt something was missing.

Finally, fate, or destiny (or the universe) had to intervene to enable me to see what playing bigger meant for me. The guide that led me to find my purpose came in the form of my fledgling yoga practice. Focusing my mind on my body and breath enabled me to tunnel into the dark places where I had hidden my dream to be a writer. Time on the mat allowed me to boldly consider that I was no less and no more worthy than anyone else to shine a light on that particular creative pursuit. More important, I learned that I was compelled to write. I had things to say, and it was time to voice them. I would not be putting books into the hands of young girls (my original business plan), but I would be pushing on the world to make that happen, and my words were my most powerful tool.

A chance conversation with a friend revealed that she, too, had always wanted to write. That was our simple, scary truth. We founded the Mandala Writers Circle, a group of two and only two. We told no one except our husbands at first; it was all too fragile to be subjected to the aspersions that others might cast on the idea of either of us writing seriously. The pact was that together we could stare down our fear and self-doubt and hold each other accountable for producing our best work. To put it more bluntly, we would not allow the other to run away from her dream of creating.

It has been a period of revelation for me. This idea has stuck because I am not alone, and I have nothing to prove. Two years in, I am not bored or worried that this writing thing will run its course and I will need to find a new avocation. Writing feels like a journey with many paths and lookout points, and at each new rise in the trail I see vistas to explore. And, unlike the world of commerce, there is no writing problem I am unable to resolve with my own heart and mind and soul.

As thoughtful and pragmatic people muddling through this new century, we search, we seek, and then we tell ourselves life is about all the other pressing concerns. We quiet the voice that says that what we are doing each day does not feed our souls. We come to believe that those times when we are filled up with creativity and ideas and contentment and joy, when we are living outside of time and limits and mundane concerns, are meant to be fleeting. The real business of life, we say, is having things and experiences and jobs and progeny. But if we are lucky, if we are paying attention, if we are courageous, we might be able to see life's exquisite mystery differently. We might see a vision for our lives and then use our talents in service of that calling. There are many questions, and there is no clear path. It is so much easier to turn away from, instead of toward, the opportunity before us.

Inhale. Pause. Exhale. The answer for each of us lies in the quiet space between breaths.

ON CLARITY
CHILD'S POSE, BALASANA

Kneel on your mat with your knees apart. Bend forward so that your forehead rests on the mat and your buttocks rest on or close to your heels. Stretch your arms out in front of you, palms down. Feel the release as your limbs and muscles let go of holding you up, and give in to gravity. At any time in your practice when you feel overwhelmed, return to child's pose and to yourself.

I almost do not go to yoga that day, my first day, because I am afraid it will be awkward. Everyone else will be really good at it, I think, or really old—and really good at it. I throw on my ratty yoga pants and I go because I remember that this is a commitment I have made to myself, and no one else cares if I ever find my way to the mat. The room is warm, the teacher is kind, the yoga is gentle. Even child's pose is difficult, as I am stiff and tight and hurting. I find stillness in myself, though, just for a moment. In the final resting period, or Savasana, I have a vision of a golden Chinese character, spinning above my head, and I want it to stay there forever.

Two weeks later, I lose my job. It's a strange expression, to lose one's job. I know exactly where the job is, and I suspected the layoff was coming. Still, it feels bad to be caught in a downsizing and to give up that comforting sense of control over my own destiny. I am no longer part of that place and that group, I no longer catch the train each morning, I no longer go out for coffee at 3 o'clock each afternoon. That job and this Me are separated, but nothing has been lost. I am curled safely around myself to absorb the blow to my ego. I am in the place where I have the chance to discover who I am and who I could be. I am free.

I go back to my yoga class. No one there knows what my role is in life, or anything else about me. In fact, those concepts seem unimportant in that warm, darkened room. I am a yogini, a seeker, a practitioner. I am on a journey with no clear destination, an astronaut into my own internal space. It is so peaceful in this universe, so secure. I realize I rarely feel safe anymore. At middle age I have become plagued by anxiety about small and big things: whether the restaurant will have a table for us, whether my daughters will be happy and fulfilled, whether the rape and killing and atrocities will ever stop. But in the studio those thoughts fall away, and I am left with just me and my mat; we are working on something together, and, instead of creating fear, it is exhilarating.

I have been here before, on the verge of a new adventure, feeling free and excited and scared. Fifteen years ago, I abruptly walked away from a successful corporate career. My reasons were burdens that became imperatives. I longed to spend more time with my two young daughters, I had an entrepreneurial itch to scratch, and I was grieving the loss of my mother who died too young. I was out of sorts and felt disconnected from my own life. I had to make a change.

What followed was a busy decade of parenting and consulting, of straddling both worlds and trying to get closer to what was important. I bumped up against it a few times, but a life's purpose is a skittish creature, something you might see in your peripheral vision but cannot quite assign a name or shape. Practical concerns won out invariably, and I found myself back in the corporate world when the offer to return to structure and financial gain was too good.

For me, corporate life is something like I imagine indentured servitude must be, at least for the soul. It requires belief in the importance of things that will not necessarily make the world a better place. This might be working for months on the specifications for a product that is ultimately scrapped. Or solving the same customer service problem every day. It might mean tolerating the bullying behavior of an executive who is carelessly destroying the firm. These endeavors were critical enough for me to rise before dawn, to rush and stress and sweat, and to sacrifice my time and attention for years. After three decades, I have put in the proverbial 10,000 hours required to make me an expert in my field. But, it's been a lopsided bargain in that all that expertise-building made it too easy to shut out any uninvited appearances of my calling. Five years later, I am kneeling on a yoga mat like a child and getting a fix on what that might be.

The strongest urge was to share my love of reading with a wider world. I knew that a large part of the world's female population was never educated and never taught to read. It seemed to me that if more people could read, we could heal many of the terrible wounds in our collective society. Where to start, though. I didn't know anything about philanthropy except for the frustrating experiences I had had sitting on non-profit boards. What I knew was business. I decided to launch a socially responsible company that would fund an educational non-profit. Sales of sustainable and eco-friendly women's fashion accessories would give me entrée into a world I knew only as a consumer, and a portion of proceeds would fund my reading-for-all philanthropy. I plunged in, buoyed by friends and colleagues who were also trying on new vocations, and together we attended entrepreneurs' workshops and networking group meetings. I did the research and wrote up the artifacts that support a business. I kept seeing obstacles in front of me—how to build a website, how to market the company, how to structure the business model, how to find suppliers—and then knocking them down. My last hurdle was to marry my model of selling with technology that would support it and to do it all for almost no investment. As it so often does, life stepped in, this time in the form of a family crisis; I put my plans aside to be there for my family for as long as it took.

In the months that passed while I stepped away, I admitted to myself that, although my idea was a good one and probably sound from a business perspective, leading a start-up felt like a burden instead of an exhilarating ride. I still believe, fiercely, that the world has to change in fundamental ways, but I was not ready to become an ecommerce entrepreneur. In fact, this endeavor started to feel like a distraction from my original goal of educating women. I was a bit embarrassed to admit this to my friends and loved ones, those who had listened endlessly and excitedly to my ideas and plans. These moments cause us shame and guilt, and I have had my share. There is a part of me that believes that a successful person sees every idea through to completion, and that because I regularly have ideas and only take them so far, I am not as successful as I might be.

Putting my plans on hold gave me the chance to reconsider what drives us and what makes us pull back. I could see that while I was running very fast toward something—a cool idea, a worthy vision—I was also furiously putting distance between me and something else. I was suspended in the middle, stopped in my tracks. This limbo was a familiar feeling, along with a sense of unease about what I was leaving behind. If I was going to finally explore it, I had to start running back, to myself.

I found it easiest to fire up my latent consulting practice. I was reminded in the first engagement of skills I had honed in the last five years of working in a company: what I am called to do for work is to help others solve their business problems. I meet with business leaders as individuals or in groups and we sort through their latest roadblocks, or hash out new plans, or work to understand the motivations of others and the political environment that they each must navigate. I serve as a coach and facilitator, doing more listening than talking, asking questions that bring us closer to root causes and wayward paths. It is easy for me to help them, as it would be easy for them to help me; having distance from a problem, and claiming no ownership of that problem or responsibility for it, is a luxury.

I walk into each meeting with a conscious intention: please let me listen well enough so that I can figure out what is really going on. Shutting off the little voice in my head that wants to judge my client takes practice and vigilance. We are all flawed. Leaders may be misguided. It is easy to jump to assumptions and pat answers, but problems are rarely one-dimensional, and the human element makes them remarkably complex. I work to provide my clients with frameworks within which they can operate. They yearn for parameters and to be told that everything is fixable. Beautifully, sometimes unaccountably, they learn from their mistakes.

What keeps me hooked on this kind of work are the moments of grace I see in those offices and conference rooms. A senior leader will publicly acknowledge his own culpability in the grave decision that sent his company into a free fall. A young manager will fearlessly present bad news to a room full of colleagues and defend herself without becoming defensive. An emerging leader will see that he has extraordinary gifts and that he has not yet put them to use. A coaching client will recognize that she has grown as a person, the landscape has changed, and she will never look at things in quite the same way. These individuals make me proud to be part of their lives and the lives of their companies.

I can define myself as a coach and consultant then, but that is what I do, and what I do is my vocation. All of my training and experience has developed into expertise in this field. But there is another calling too—not as insistent or sure of itself, not as credible perhaps—to write. It feels like these two should be combined, and not into something as simple as "writing about coaching." It is bigger than that, and I know it. It has to do with using my particular gifts in service of my vision. That vision is that the world is more just and compassionate, less self-centered and self-serving, more balanced and less violent. More conscious.

I see now that my life's work has been in front of me all along and that I have been actively engaged in it. What I am called to provide is clarity. Making the complex clear, shining a light on the ugly truth, putting things back in proper perspective—these are my activities. I work from a place of believing that this clarity will come but cannot be forced. I know how to do this out in the world, but have not had the courage to do this with my own voice, my own words, on the page.

You cannot always start from the beginning, but you can start from where you are. You are a student, and you will always be a student. Kneeling with your forehead on the floor and your arms outstretched in front of you, you are a child again. You will always be a child. There is humility in this. There is grace. You surrender to the limits of your body and your mind and you rebuild from there.

ON BODY AND MIND
DOWNWARD FACING DOG, ADHO MUKHA SVANASANA

Press up onto your hands and feet like an upside-down V, with your hips as the highest point. Release the effort in your shoulders. You are on four limbs, and you resemble a dog stretching itself. You are looking between your legs and behind you, at something you never noticed before. You find your drishti, or focused gaze. Your mind lifts for a moment and you sense space between your thoughts. Your perspective is irrevocably changed.

At first Down Dog is hard. It's uncomfortable to be upside down. My legs scream and my arms ache.

My mind wails that I just want it to be over. When I started yoga, my intention was simply to touch my toes. For as long as I can remember, I have been unable to effortlessly bend over and brush even the tops of my feet. There are physiological reasons for this: tight hamstrings that have taken over for weak abdominals in the effort to hold me upright. The result is the stiff and inflexible body to which I've grown accustomed. I have made accommodations for ongoing backache and the need to bend my knees to pick things up, and I assumed that this was just the type of body I had. Then a friend cautioned, "if you're this inflexible now, imagine what you'll feel like in 10 years!" I knew the body I was in, but I never thought of it getting worse. That was the motivator that got me into that first yoga class—a vision of myself moving stiffly through my life, encased in my body as I shuffled about. Call it fear. Touching my toes was a goal I threw in to make it real.

It occurs to me while upside down in Down Dog that I don't know much about where my body is in space most of the time. I never really connect with the corporeal form that I inhabit on the planet. In many ways, I take it for granted. In other ways, I find it wanting. I have all my limbs working, the systems are functioning, my vital stats are normal. There are a few aches and pains and odd cracking sounds, but nothing debilitating. There are parts that I feel are too big or too small or not shaped exactly as I might have designed them. These bother me more than I'd like to admit, believing as I do that we are all greater than the sum of our parts. But there it is. I am flawed. I am vain. I am human.

I am also not paying attention. My body is doing all of these tasks for me every day, taking whatever physical and mental abuse I throw at it, and going about its business without any guidance from me. I wonder, not for the first time, what it might be like to really understand all the parts and pieces and do a bit more directing. A ballerina can only do what she does if she is acutely aware of every part of her glorious being. The dance is a series of discrete movements strung together so precisely that we cannot see where one ends and the next begins. But the dancer knows. She is aware at every moment, pushing her body and creating with it. She is making art with her body. It is possible.

Back to toe touching. I knew it would take a while to undo the work of a lifetime of poor posture, but I didn't count on the sweat and discomfort of something as seemingly simple as Down Dog. To hold the posture, I bend and straighten my legs. I gently push my hips higher into the air and spread my shoulders to ease the pressure. I remember I am practicing, that I am learning and stretching myself. Thrust into the world with nothing but time and ideas, I am able to think and meet and attend and explore. I consider my life's purpose again. It is a fine goal to bring clarity to a confused world, but the challenge is daunting. I feel a bit overwhelmed, upside-down, a little nauseous even. My first impulse is to go do something more enjoyable.

What better way to avoid the call of duty than to curl up with a good book? If anything has contributed to the general distractedness from purpose, and failure to take the time to view my own life in new ways, it has been this: an obsessive reading habit. I suffer from an inability to stick to a single genre, a tendency to follow meandering reading wormholes, and a strong dislike of sitting idly when there must certainly be something to read nearby. As a reader, I am not very Zen-like. I hop from past to present to future aimlessly and do not stay in any one place long enough to feel its essence. For all this, I am most content when reading, and when I do not have a book to think about, I am at loose ends.

I blame my parents. My mother, an obsessive reader herself, introduced me to books as a toddler. She read to me every night and the stories varied from the charming to the frightening, from *Winnie-the-Pooh* and *Aesop's* fables to *Grimm's* fairy tales. Some we read over and over, like the stories of *The Book of One Thousand and One Nights* and Kipling's *Just So Stories*. We balanced these with other favorites, like *Ferdinand the Bull* and *Mike Mulligan and His Steam Shovel*. No book was considered too long or too scary; if I wanted to have it read to me, it was. On many nights, my father was in charge of story time, and he made up fantastic tales on the spot. My older brother and I would lie rapt on either side of him as he spun the latest installment of his "Black Jack the Pirate and the Golden Princess" series. These were fantastic tales of dragons in craggy lairs, ingenious devices, flying turtles and giant eagles, magical lands, damsels in distress, brave heroes, true love, and happily every after. My father would often drift off to sleep mid-rescue and my dreams would fill in the rest of the story.

Together, my parents built the footings for my imagination, teaching me that words could create entire worlds. They taught me about Story. I could not wait to learn to read, and I remember the moment when letters on the page formed a complete, immutable word: S-E-E. I knew instantly that all words were like this, fully formed and each invested with specific meaning. I read everything I could get my hands on, devouring series like they were cupcakes, hungry for more when the last Laura Ingalls Wilder or Frank L. Baum was finished. Reading became my escape, my teacher and friend, a place to go to relax in a busy household. After a while, it didn't matter much what I read; everything fed my knowledge or fed my imagination. I would steal sports book from my brother's room, finding as much to fascinate me in *I Am Third* and *Bang the Drum Slowly* as I had in *The Diary of Anne Frank*. No book was off limits in our house, so I discovered Scarlett O'Hara, Sherlock Holmes, and Archy and Mehitabel on the bulging shelves and ingested them all.

In my 20s I was goaded into book collecting by a Book-of-the-Month Club editor who blithely stated that "one cannot consider himself a true reader unless he's read P.G. Wodehouse." *The World of Jeeves* was my first purchase, and it only whetted my appetite. This began a decades-long quest to track down as many Wodehouse books as I could, and brought me into secondhand bookstores in cities all over the country. These 90 or so harmless farces, set in English country houses full of nitwits, are my reading candy, a guilty pleasure I return to when life seems out of sorts and needs to be set right.

Through all the chapters of my life, my appetite has not waned. My nightstand currently holds the following stack: *Rumi: Collected Poems,* Billy Collins' *Horoscopes for the Dead,* E. B. White's *Stuart Little,* Chimamanda Ngozi Adichie's *Americanah,* Blakewell's biography of Montaigne, and Joseph Campbell's *The Hero with a Thousand Faces.* Waiting in the wings is Wallace Stegner's *Crossing to Safety,* due shortly for book group. When I have ploughed through that, I'll treat myself to a mystery or two, to clear my reading palate. I am always hungry for more Dorothy L. Sayers, P.D. James, Louise Penny, and Jacqueline Winspear. I'll incorporate this last meal into the bookcases, archive them in my Kindle, and make way for new (to me) writers and thinkers, new worlds. I rarely read books a second time, but cannot seem to let any of them go. I barely remember the specifics of anything I've read, but retain a sense of both how it felt to read it and who among my friends would most enjoy it.

No one will shame you for reading too much, but I wonder sometimes about my habit's purpose. I have been a collector of information—disparate facts, magical places, extraordinary characters—all my life. Like walking around in a body I hardly consider, my mind is going about its business of absorbing the jumbled mess of sweet and savory words with little connection to vocation or avocation. It is a lovely way to escape, but no way to live. Prone on the sofa with legs and head propped, in the reader's Down Dog so to speak, I look up from the current book just long enough to consider that I am nourished by reading but never sated. I hold the thought. I write it down.

ON HIDING
VINYASA FLOW

From Down Dog, lower your hips and move forward so that your shoulders are directly over your hands and your feet are straight out behind you, toes on the mat. You are in a Plank pose, one straight line from heels to head. Your arms are straight, your abdominals are taut. Tighten the muscles in your buttocks, thighs and calves. Your feet are flexed as if they are standing on the wall behind you. Feel the richness here; you are holding up the universe. You are a superhero in flight.

I remember when I first understood what writing meant and how I could use words in powerful ways. I was in 6th grade. Our assignment was to write a fictional story. This was 1973 and the evening news was filled with the anguish of the Vietnam War. My town honored a returned POW with a big parade, a bright spot in a dark and confusing time. I was too young to understand war and its causes, or imprisonment and its effects. I understood, though, that these things meant loss and sadness at some universal level. I decided to write my story about a young girl whose brother dies in Vietnam. The plot escapes me, but I remember comparing the girl's sense of loss and the finality of death to "a sandcastle when the tide comes in." Something beautiful and innocent is destroyed by the harsh and relentless ocean; brothers are lost to the exigencies of war. I got it. I made the words do it. It was thrilling. The pen was my sword, and I had full control over it. It was like having a super power.

My teacher, Mr. Sisson, whom I adored, saw this power as well. He did everything he could to nurture it. He gently critiqued my pieces, serving as a fine editor, giving his writer the lead. He typed out 30 or 40 opening paragraphs for stories and on the last day of school pressed them on me, encouraging me to spend the summer playing with them. I promised him that I would continue to write in junior high. One day that fall a package arrived. It was a hardcover book for young readers, published by an author in town. The note atop it from Mr. Sisson said he had met her and shown her my work and had her inscribe her book for me. I still have it on my bookshelf. "To Leah Carey—" it reads, "a very talented young lady. May the promise be fulfilled."

From Plank, lower your body by bending your elbows, keeping them close to your sides. Keep all the elements of taut strength and hover inches above the floor. This is Low Plank or Chaturanga Dandasana, part of the sun salutation. You are four limbs and a staff (your backbone). You are a corporeal being, flesh and bone.. You bow to the sun.

I did not write anything that summer, and I put the story leads back in their envelope. I dabbled a bit over the next few years, experimenting with terrible poetry in pretty journals, shying away from anything that might seem like I was really writing. I felt a lot of pressure to be very, very good at something I had just discovered. It was easier to become a technician than to excavate my heart, so I focused on the craft and left the mystery alone. I loaded up on English courses and solved the riddle of the critical essay. I won a writing award at my high school on graduation day. I became an English major in college ostensibly because I loved to read. I wrote pages and pages of opinion and critique, showing my understanding of other writers, mostly male, mostly dead. In my senior year I was told by the Office of Career Planning and Placement that, given I was an English major, I should not expect to get a job. I set out to prove them wrong. By April I had an offer in hand, and by June I found myself in a bank management training program.

People who know me well find it amusing that I went into banking at all. It is a structured, generally bureaucratic, and heavily policy-driven line of work. For me at 22, it meant a secure job, a career path, and a better salary than anyone else was offering. It gave me bragging rights, and that was what it was all about in the money-driven 1980s. I discovered other things there as well, like strong and confident leaders, recognition, opportunities to try new things, and a group of people my age who were smart and driven and fun. It honed my ability to compartmentalize, too, and I learned to keep my work life and my personal life separate and to put the development of my inner life on hold. I started then to create my work persona as a refuge.

On the last day of that intensive six-month training program, my group of 17 colleagues and I met in the boardroom with our leader. I took in the view of the sparkling city and dreamed about my future sitting there as an executive. I looked around the table at my good friends and felt happy and accomplished. Our surprise assignment that day was simple: share something with the group that no one else in the room knows about you. I had no idea what I would say. My mind raced as the talking stick slowly made its way toward me. My panic grew as I listened. One woman spoke about her sister, who had recently come out as a lesbian. My closest friend admitted to us all that she had a medical condition for which there was no cure. Another said his brother had committed suicide as a teenager. These were stories of loss, and these people were unburdening themselves. In public. Around the room it went, story after story of trials and heartbreak.

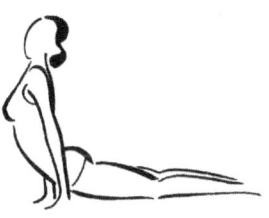

Roll forward over your toes, drop your hips and lift your head. Keep your arms straight, arch your back, lift your thighs off the mat. In Upward-Facing Dog, salute the sun with your shining radiance. Open your heart. Find what is true for you right now, at this moment.

My panic returned. I had nothing to share. When the room turned to me, I told them the story of my early writing success a decade earlier, my teacher, the inscription in the book and "may the promise be fulfilled." I left that room feeling ashamed that I had not had the same courage as the others had, that I had provided a bit of fluff at the last minute because I was so afraid to trust them with something truly important. But still, I could not think of what that something important might be.

I see now, 30 years later, that I did share my one truth. I shared my super power, let them peek at the cape and the tights. But the timing was off, and it had seemed cheap and tawdry to speak about something good in light of their pain. Besides, I was not even sure if it was true about me. What had I written? What had I done with the promise? So I had a secret power and yet I didn't use it. Did that make me a fraud, or simply weak? I buried the day, buried the memory, buried the gift. I went about my business in street clothes and worked very hard to never have to jump into the proverbial phone booth and save the world.

Push back on your heels, raise your hips, return to Down Dog. Exhale, you have completed the flow. Observe. Breathe deeply. Return yourself to yourself. Begin again.

ON SELF-DOUBT
COBRA POSE, BHUJANGASANA

From Down Dog, shift forward to plank and then lower yourself to your mat. Lie on your stomach with your elbows bent and your palms flat on the ground next to your lower ribs. Push the toenail side of your feet so firmly onto the mat that your knees lift off the ground. From this taut stance, tighten your lower abdomen and lift your chest off the floor, so that you are slightly arched and staring straight ahead. Hold this posture and feel its power. You are a cobra, ready to strike.

Given the choice, I do not choose to do Cobra in yoga class. For me, the glorious Upward Dog with its heart-opening stance always feels right. Sometimes the choice is not given, and Cobra is what we practice. It is not comfortable to me and feels incomplete, like a half a pose. It is necessary though for back strengthening, a core posture. I can learn from Cobra even if I do not like it, but I cannot entirely avoid it, any more than I can avoid the cobra in my life.

The hissing starts quietly. I hear whispers, "you should lose weight" or "you are a bad mother" or "you are not that smart" or "your writing is terrible, stop it now!". I may not notice them at first, so they become louder or more incessant. A steady droning blocks out my creativity and rationality so that all I hear is the hisshisshiss of self-loathing. The cobra is the voice that says I can't do it. The cobra says I probably screwed up that meeting, it was something I said. The cobra tells me I'm not likable. The cobra says I can't have that dream, and if I could, I would have made it happen by now. The cobra tells me not to bother voicing my intention in the universe because I won't follow through anyway. The cobra says it will be too difficult, that I don't know how to do it, that it's too complicated, that no one will support me and I will be alone. The cobra says other people are better at that skill and I have no business stepping into the arena with them.

The cobra smells like the acrid smoke of fear. The stench and the fangs and the hood come out when I am close to knowing a new truth about myself, when

I am just about to enter the cave of discovery. The cobra is the dragon that stands in the way, writhing and spitting and venomous, protecting its treasure, the me who is yet to be. The cobra makes me jump back, and back off. The cobra makes me take it personally. The cobra looks like an ancient, mythological monster and makes me feel small.

The cobra is me.

The cobra was there when Mr. Sisson urged me to write in 6th grade, and hissed at me when I became tongue-tied in that boardroom of shared truths so long ago. I know the snake bit me in the interview I blew at Very Important University and made me a pile of nerves before going on stage to present to executives the first time. I thought I had wrestled those vipers back into their lairs. But just before the writer's retreat I attended to focus solely on this book, I was attacked by the cobras I had conjured on my own. I heard every negative thought—bad mother, bad daughter, bad sister, bad friend, bad writer, and on and on—until I had convinced myself that I was not competent to write at all because I had nothing of value to say. This time, though, something was different. I had the ability to write about what I felt even if I did not know what it meant. In writing about the cobra, I was able to see it and separate from it.

What I learned is that my powerful and sinuous ego is like the king cobra that makes a nest for its eggs and remains until the young hatch. It protects. It wants me not to be hurt. It wants to conserve the status quo, to babysit the nest. Most of the time, I have no awareness of my ego threatening me to stay as I am. I am generally a content and fulfilled person, curious about the world, seeking adventure. It is when I stray from the path and reach beyond my perceived limits that I sense the hiss and the venom. It is as if it has emerged from its hiding place and slithered into my mind's periphery. Until I charm this serpent, I will be at its mercy, too afraid to cross its path, too afraid to step beyond my vision of myself.

The writers' retreat was a success because I could see my self-doubt for what it was. Sitting in my room that first night, I was filled with relief and joy. I knew that if the cobra attack was so extreme, I must be on the verge of something exciting. I thought of the Zen koan, *how do you go further from the top of a 100-foot pole?* and had an answer: we leap into doubt. This jump into the unknown is powerful and frightening; it makes your heart race and your palms sweat. It is exactly what your ego does not want you to do.

I have three choices in snake charming: sew the mouth shut and ultimately starve the ego to death; worship it and let it own my soul; or treat my cobra-ego with respect and thereby honor its essential nature. That is, I can allow the ego to have its say and to demand my attention while also standing my ground. When the cobra strikes again, I must recognize the fangs: the harsh criticism, the feeling of aching loneliness, the paralyzing self-doubt. I will then lay the snake across my shoulders, ask it to keep a lookout in the darkness with its unblinking eyes, let it slither through the cave before me, and listen without fear to its interpretation of the symbols etched on the walls. Once tamed, it can coil itself in a dark corner and leave me to find the way forward on my own.

ON INTENTION
MOUNTAIN POSE, TADASANA

Push up from Cobra into Upward Dog, then lift your hips and return to Down Dog. Walk your feet forward, placing them hip distance apart between your hands, and slowly roll to standing.. Feel the four corners of your feet pressing into the earth. Feel your calves over your ankles, your thighs over your calves, your hips and pelvis atop your legs. Feel the strength and symmetry. Stack your ribcage over your hips and your neck above your back. Hold your chin parallel to the floor. Put your arms at

your sides, palms facing forward, fingers spread. Feel the power in your beautiful body, the joy it gives you in standing on the ground, the space it creates for you. You are a mountain, teeming with life. Now, set your intention for your practice.

If I approach my life as if I am simply standing on the mat, then I have missed the point. We are never just standing because we are alive. But living means I must have intent. What will I do with my time? What will I share with the world? Who will I be with? Who will I be without? We start each class setting an intention for it, a way that we want to be while we are on our mats. It might be gratitude or love, or kindness or creativity or peace or joy. The intention itself is true because it is mine and I choose it. In Mountain Pose, I revisit the intention, just as in the quiet spaces in my life I remember that I am alive—tingling, teeming, standing, being—and that this is enough, more than enough.

I was very much alive in all those years between starting in banking and finding myself on a yoga mat. I was working hard for others and then for myself, carving out a niche as a leadership expert and corporate coach. I was mindfully mothering two daughters and helping them to understand the world around them. I was loving my husband and co-creating a life that would extend far beyond the parenting years.

My intention in those years was simply to be curious. Work was challenging and often fulfilling.

Outside of work, I found myself in classrooms and assisting in theater productions, sitting on non-profit boards and in committee meetings, and swapping stories and confidences with good friends. I read hundreds of books and wrote thousands of emails. The Internet sated my hunger for information and opinion. I traveled across continents and oceans.

The years flew by, as they do, captured in photos and in my heart. Those memories and the learning made their way to the surface at the end of each year; I would write a holiday letter to our family and friends to share the view from my corner of the world. "You must write," friends would say each new year, "we want to hear more." There were fits and starts—essays and poems, travelogues, a first chapter for a children's book, a blog post or two—and all were safely squirreled away for some other, better time. I never could find that time, though. Each year had its new distractions and adventures, and those were joyously welcomed because I was terribly afraid.

The thing about fear is it's one thing to see it and name it and give it a place at your side. It's much harder to understand it. I am not sure what I was so very afraid of then. Of course, there is always the fear the work will not be good enough. For whom, I am not sure. Then, there is the fear that the work will be good, and I might have to change my life. Maybe that success would mean I would be regarded differently by others—those who know me well and those who don't, those I care for deeply and those I do not care about at all. Maybe success would mean I would have to define myself differently—call myself a writer—and deliver on that implicit promise. Maybe it would mean that I would have to write every day and produce something of value without fail from one sunrise to the next. Maybe I would have to give up other things that bring me out into the world. Maybe it would be lonely in my garret. Maybe it would change me. Maybe.

I have run away from writing when I have read other works that were so good—so lyrical, so authentic, so exactly what I was thinking—that it felt pointless to add my small voice to the conversation. I have fled when someone else wrote "my book," told what felt like my story. I have shied away when people told me I should write, asked me why I don't write, given me books about writing and beautiful pens and knowing nods. Even now I must force myself to write, schedule it like all my other must do's and then feel guilty about it when I do not get down to it. How much can it be a calling if I do not feel compelled? It is not the first priority, the one around which all other must-do's must settle and find their place. I am still sheepish about it, guarding writing like a secret. When someone asks what I am writing, I stumble over the words, and the whole enterprise sounds lifeless and uninspiring.

I am not alone. There are many, many books about writing, and they are not all about technique. A good portion of these writers-on-writing simply offer encouragement. They gently urge the writer to get down to business, showing us those who have gone before us and survived, telling us that it will be okay. It is hard to imagine that doctors, engineers, factory workers, painters, or dancers need so much urging to do what they do. What is it about writing that we shy away from?

What books-about-writing misunderstand is that to call it writing is too broad. It is an activity, not a noble pursuit in itself, at least for me. Just "to write," then, is equal to all other to do's: to work, to parent, to cook, to clean. Writing has to have a purpose; to share a story and in it a point of view; to share a point of view and in it a philosophy; to share a philosophy and in it a story. If my life's purpose is attained through writing, then writing is a means to an end, not an end in itself.

Writing is not the mountain, but the means to scale it. Writing is hiking boots and a walking stick, a day pack and trail mix, the essentials that help us on the journey. Sometimes the voice of doubt drives me down the mountain, but I need to keep climbing. My mountain pose is my purpose, my intention to make things clear for myself and others. I will have to move forward with writing even when it may feel like I am standing still. When I am afraid, I need to find Tadasana and stand in my power. I will have to get grounded when every part of me wants to fly away.

ON CONQUERING FEAR
WARRIOR I, VIRABHADRASANA I

From Tadasana, fold forward and place your hands on the floor beside your feet. Reach your left foot behind you and bend your right knee so you are in a runner's lunge. Turn your left foot so that it is flat on the mat and at a forty-five degree angle. Your feet are now a leg's distance apart and your heels are in a straight line. Inhale, and slowly bring your torso to vertical. Your arms reach up, your shoulder blades slide down your

back, your pinkies turn slightly toward each other. Your legs stay as they are, and your hips are turned toward the front of your mat. There is a delicate pressure as your bent right knee reaches forward and your straight left leg tugs backward. Your weight is placed as much as possible on your left leg; your left foot presses firmly on the floor, and your left thigh and buttock are completely engaged. You are standing with purpose and you are poised to strike. Your heart shines forward. You are a warrior ready for battle. Exhale.

The early moments of a yoga class can be peaceful or agitated, and the energy of those in the room determines which way it will be. Sometimes I enter a fairly empty studio and those there before me are quietly stretching on their mats. Other times, I arrive while the room is filling up and there is some jockeying for space, lots of movement, and the low hum of voices. In either case, I work to stake out my territory because I am wary of distractions. I prefer to be in a front corner, where I can be alone with my thoughts and the walls and tune out whatever anyone else has brought into the room.

One day I did not arrive early enough to anchor myself by a wall, so I was adrift in the middle of the room, caught up in the arrivals around me. An older gentleman came in just as class started. Rather than recognize our peaceful collective Child's Pose, he announced loudly that he had forgotten his mat. The teacher deftly kept the drama to a minimum as the gentleman noisily worked to situate himself front and center. The need for attention reverberated off of him, and anyone near him could not help but be thrown off. We pushed into a tabletop position, then Down Dog, then into Mountain Pose. As I stood in my Tadasana, still shrugging off the earlier distraction, another woman quietly joined the group. The only space for her was at the front of the room, perpendicular to the teacher. She carefully placed her props and mat and became a mountain before my eyes. Within seconds, it was as if she had always been there. More than that, she made the room complete.

I was witnessing ego and grace, acting out and acting in, and balancing each other. It was almost as if they neutralized each other. As we moved into Warrior I and I found my center, I had the startling realization that the Ego-man was not separate from me, that he was in fact a piece of me, the piece that is easily annoyed by tiny things and sometimes embarrassed to be late or unprepared. I have to work hard not to be like him on some days. Grace-woman is easy to love. I want to be like her all the time, but she is harder to emulate. She is also a part of me, the part that seeks to understand and to create space for others. In fact everyone in the class reflects something about myself back to me, and I to them. Some seek solitude and inner peace, some are looking for physical challenges, some want to show off, and some prefer to keep to themselves. In any given class, on any given day, I can be any or all of those people.

Perhaps, I wondered, this is the beginning of true compassion. Before that moment, I thought compassion was being able to feel sympathy for the struggling newcomer, or concern for the out-of-shape woman who falls over, or admiration for the octogenarian who never misses a class. Compassion seemed like something noble, maybe an advanced level of empathy. Compassion, I see now, is the recognition that everyone else is just another piece of the whole mystery. If I tune them out, I have tuned myself out. If I think of them as separate, I am separate. If I honor them, I honor me.

This shift in perspective is like the rarest of birds, beautiful to behold but difficult to capture. These higher truths tease us, flitting about as we remain rooted in our own reality. I was raised to face the world as a proud warrior: an open heart, poised to defend my honor. As a result, I can be at war with others at times. They irritate me, I make assumptions about them, and sometimes I secretly seek to be them. Moreover, I can be at war with myself. I become frustrated, I criticize, and then I humbly recognize and forgive my flaws. I can be so judgmental, so quick to sum up a person or situation in a sound bite. Yet this is the flip side of my critical thinking skill, the thing that allows me to walk into any business situation and quickly assess and provide solutions. I treasure my ability, but dislike its dark side. I need a way to allow my ego to breathe before I snap to judgment. I wonder what the Warrior I is for my soul when I cannot be on the mat.

Perhaps it is to write, to write what I believe. To turn those judgments into observation, analysis, and commentary, and in so doing make sense of them for myself and for others. It sounds easy, but to put my principles and beliefs on paper, for me, is to march onto the battlefield. Like a soldier, I fear for my life. Like a warrior, I believe it is what I must do.

Standing in Warrior I, I am at the moment before the battle begins. I am more excited than afraid. I feel the harsh wind that slices across the plain. I see the enemy fires and know they are ones I lit long ago: doubt, fear, anger, shame. There will be victories, and there will be casualties I will face whatever comes head on, ready with my shining heart, poised and full of compassion.

ON SELF-CONFIDENCE
WARRIOR II, VIRABHADRASANA II

As you stand in Warrior I with your left leg forward, keep your legs as they are and gracefully turn your hips to the right. Open your arms so that they reach straight out from your shoulders. Keep your shoulders level by pulling down on your shoulder blades. Sit even further into the posture. Look over your left middle finger and focus your gaze, your drishti. Find your center. Find your purpose.

When I am in Warrior II, I feel that I have summoned all the power in my body and have directed it at a single point in the far distance. I feel strong, even fierce. I feel as if the years have fallen away and I am my young self, full of potential and fire. In Virabhadrasana II I am every girl, every female who commands her space, who is open to possibility, who is unafraid.

The uniform begins with a ponytail, smooth and tight. It is the most practical method of keeping the hair off the face. What you see is the whole girl, fully exposed to the world. Short hair would be easier, but it would reduce one's choices. These girls like to keep their options open. These girls are not concerned with how they look on the field. For practice, any old tee shirt will do. Standard-issue nylon shorts are worn long or rolled at the top. Lean thighs stop at knee socks stretched around shin guards. Cleats are required. A water bottle is essential. The effect is clean, athletic, unadorned.

They arrive at practice by car, by bicycle, or aboard a scooter. They are there to play, both the game and with each other. They are fit because they play. They are good at what they do. They rely on each other to handle what comes—to think, to react, to strategize. They call out each other's names to pass and throw in, they slap hands together as they sub out, they charge and push as necessary, they apologize when they are too rough.

They swagger off the field. From a distance, it is hard to distinguish one daughter from another; they look so much alike in their gear. They are sweaty and grubby. They smell like hard work. Someone starts a water fight. They do not notice the golden glow of the late afternoon sun or how it shines in their hair. They do not know that at this most mundane of moments they are ethereal, a band of giggling, bouncing angels with swishing tails. Their self-assurance is breathtaking.

They are the girls we never were. Growing up on their own fields, confident and strong, playing with abandon. For them, there are no relative terms. They do not compare themselves to boys, to the generations when there were no girls' sports, to the mores and expectations of an earlier time. This is not all they do or all they are or all they will be. This is practice; the game comes later. They are soccer girls.

I wrote this piece 10 years ago, when my girls were young and soccer was their universe. I saw them then as I see them now: they are beautiful warriors. They each show up for the game every day, and it is not easy to do that in this world. They surprise me with their choices and delight me with their courage. They love to be with me and they are happy to be away. They are sisters who look and act so different from each other that they may never have found each other if they were not related. They are friends first and last. I have learned more about being a warrior from my daughters than I ever knew was possible. They taught me how to love someone so fiercely that you would breathe fire to protect her. They taught me that I had to learn to live with worry, but I could not let it erode my heart.

Some of us arrive at our purpose early in life, and some of us have to grow into it. Being a parent, being a wife, having a career, these were all essential lessons to be mastered along my path of self-discovery. I once led with my heart, but I did not think it would serve me on the battlefield, so I made my mind my shield. My intuition is strong, but I do not always trust it. I regularly resist its wisdom, defaulting to what I know and see to guide me.

Learning to feel deeply is difficult for an intellectual. It has been the work of a lifetime just to keep my focus, my *drishti*, despite the distractions of success and loss, joy and heartache, love and death. But now, my whole self—that messy amalgamation of heart and mind—has been called up to the front. I have things to say, and I must say them, whatever the consequences. My two warrior-daughters, more than anyone, taught me to look over my shoulder and point to where I want to go. They taught me to take the field.

ON PARENTING
HUMBLE WARRIOR, BADDHA VIRABHADRASANA

Shift back into Warrior I, turning your hips to face forward and raising your arms above you. Now lower your arms and clasp your hands behind you, fingers meshed, palms pressed together. Bend over forward, leaning as far as you can toward your front knee, allowing your joined arms to rise up behind you. If you can, bring your forehead to the floor. You are the humble warrior, who, bowing deeply, lays down her sword.

There is no greater personal trial than being a parent. Every sinew, every organ, every cell is tested. These tests come slowly, though, and you build your strength. First a baby cries and you must decipher her needs. A toddler gets an ear infection or whooping cough, and you must learn to discern and diagnose. A young athlete breaks a bone out on the field and you must triage and learn the internal workings of a hospital emergency room. A 10-year-old must have surgery and your worry brings you right to the edge of rationality, begging any higher power to let it go well so you can take her home. A middle-schooler is turned out by his group of friends, and you must reassure him he is not alone. A teenager gets entangled in a first love affair and you must watch for the signs of an unhealthy relationship—with a boyfriend or girlfriend, or with alcohol, or with drugs. You must be there to hold your child close as you rage at fate, other kids, or his or her choices.

As each event unfolded, I drew on what I learned the last time, but it was never quite enough. I had to stretch beyond my known world and enter a new one, with few skills and only my gut to guide me. Imagine sending a warrior into battle with no weapons or body armor and little training, and telling her to rely on her intuition. Tell her that she must then do battle to protect the most important treasures in her universe. This is the naïve gamble of parenting. Humbled by my own inexperience, I would stride naively into combat.

Parents get battle scars. Sometimes the trials are too great. Words cannot be unsaid or unheard, one-sided unconditional love can feel like an imperfect bargain, our children become adults we cannot always understand. More than once I have found myself in situations I would never have written into my life story, brought there by my children. Some were moments of indescribable joy and some were moments of wretched despair. Moment by moment they were part of my own journey. Bit by bit they have left marks on me.

I look at the blemishes on my body, the freckles and moles, the scar from a childhood ice skating accident, the burn from a camping fire. They are part of me, but they do not define me. After much practice, my scarred and imperfect body can drape forward into Humble Warrior. The imperfections of my flesh do not hold me back. So it is with my spirit. The nicks and cuts are small compared to the exquisite gift that half a lifetime of parenting has been.

The things we did. The places we went! There was learning, teaching, laughing, crying, dancing, cheering, celebrating. There were traditions, family times, family dinners, family friends. There were stories and hugs and misunderstandings and apologies. There were mistakes and successes, planning and serendipity. Through it all, there was love, the shining heart of parenting. Love so powerful it can make you walk into the fire for someone else, to do battle armed with only your wits to keep you safe.

I want my girls to see what I see in them—the grace, the intelligence, the talent, the quirks, the humor. I want them to come to understand what they each offer to the world and to know that such an offering is unique and valuable and necessary. I want them to know that their contributions, no matter how insignificant they may seem, if given with selflessness and integrity, move the world forward. I want them to know that they are not perfect, that they will never be perfect, that no one is perfect. I want them to be a part of the world, to not allow fear to hold them back, to ignore the naysayers and their inner critics and do what they think they cannot do. I want them to take the risk of being vulnerable so that they can deeply love a partner, their family, their friends, themselves.

I am cowed by both my love and my concern for my girls. I want them never to feel pain, never to be hurt, always to be happy. These are impossible goals, like wanting to avoid all casualties in a war. The best I have been able to do is to arm them with the protections they will need to fully live their own lives. When either of my adult daughters says she is coming home to visit, I cannot wait to see her. I hug her tight and listen with wonder as she tells me all about her life, her struggles and trials, her victories. I am her friend and confidante, wise in different ways, but no more or less than she is. There is no end to parenting, but there is an end to doing battle. The humble warrior, bowing deeply to the luminous soul before her, lays down her arms.

ON FRIENDSHIP
TRIANGLE POSE, TRIKONASANA

Move back into Warrior II, with arms extended to the sides. Now, straighten your bent, forward leg. Lean toward this front leg, thrusting your opposite hip back. When you have reached forward as far as you can, lower your front arm onto your leg so that it rests gently and comfortably on your calf or foot or the floor. Reach the other arm above you and turn your chest outward so that you create a straight line from lower to upper

arm. Gaze up at your fingers. You are isosceles, or scalene, or equilateral, your own unique connection to the earth, to yourself, and to the world around you.

I am continually reminded of the importance of connection in our lives, and increasingly I believe it is the only important thing. We make our way through this life with the aid of others. Each connection begins with us, goes out and comes back. We expand and contract our triangle of connection over a lifetime, sometimes able to be wide and encompassing of many connections and sometimes small and tightly bound. Connections are broken, sometimes irrevocably. We are changed, always irrevocably.

Our first connections outside of our family are our friends. Their appearance in our lives is largely a mystery. There are some friends with whom I can remember the precise moment we first met and others whose origin story is hazy. "How did we meet?" we'll say, as if it's a wonder we ever met at all. A lifelong friend and I were four when we happened on each other at swim lessons at the Y. Another close friend approached me at a Brownie troop meeting because her daughter and I share the same name. A friend in whom I can confide my deepest fears met me with a casual wave atop the roof she was helping to replace. These origin stories and others delight me with their certain beginnings. But many of my friends seemed to have appeared spontaneously in my life, at important times, or right when I needed them.

I have become who I am because of my friends, made and lost over a lifetime, every one of them teaching me essential things. They have shown me how to be thoughtful, what to bring, how it's done, how to live well. They've helped me avoid traps and have shown me how to reassemble my life at times. Because of them, I know how to recover from loss, how to recognize false friends and takers, how to parent, how to be a daughter, how to pay attention. It is with my friends that I can see my own worst qualities reflected back with love, that I have learned to accept my quirks, and that I have figured out how to dress my body. Because of them I know how to retreat, how to laugh so hard I cannot breathe, and how to cry in public. Through them I have learned to feel another's pain, to experience complete joy for someone else, and how to protect another soul. Friends have made me whole, a more complete being. More than anything, my friends have taught me gratitude.

Friends have loved me when I am hard to love and looked past my flaws when they were awkwardly on display. They have helped me laugh at myself and have shown me what is seriously good about me. Without trying, they have revealed truths about the world and helped me make sense of it. The best ones have stood by me when the path I am taking makes them confused or uncomfortable.

My friends are so giving that I sometimes struggle to know how to return their kindnesses. The same listening heart they turn to me, I turn to them. I work to solve their problems with them and to carry their burdens. Even if my life is harried, I know that time with them will enrich me and we will make each other laugh. We walk, go out to dinner, spend long weekends in new cities, celebrate birthdays, go on adventures, talk about books, and work through life's tricky parts. Though I want to give them the world, I can give them simply time and words and presence.

And yet, friends come and go. Somehow I am willing to outgrow some of them, although I would never so easily walk away from my marriage or my children or my family. Others have been cruel to me or to people I love, and I realized they must be kept at a distance. Even these few have been important, in that they were allies in making me clearly see what I believed in. It is as if friends have a greater purpose in growing me and then setting me free when they have done their part, as I do for them.

We are shape shifters as we grow and evolve, and people who fit within our triangle today may not always. There is grief in losing or even reframing these relationships, a recognition that we have changed and another person has not and now we no longer fit together as well as we once did. At these breaking points we meet guides who prepare us for the loss. They help us accept that we must shape shift, and that we know too much to stay grounded the way we are.

I met Jolene as she tumbled out of the passenger side of a van at a racetrack paddock. (My husband, Carl, is a sports car enthusiast and high-performance driving instructor, and weekends away often involve time at what we call the "pavement beach.") Jolene was so full of light and life it was palpable in the gathering dusk. "Hey you guys, want a beer?" she asked. After driving 7 hours to Canada, we had planned to drop the car off the trailer and head to the hotel. But Jolene's offer was too appealing. With her wild curly hair and big brown eyes and pixie grin, I wanted to know who she was. We caught up, she and boyfriend Dave, me and Carl, and others who found their way to our circle of laughter. It was just for an hour or so, but it was the very beginning of something.

The next day we immediately lit on a plan to go on a field trip up the road to the Scandinavian spa. I had never been to anything quite like it. It is a small Eden set in the woods, bordered by a river. Neat, barn-like structures surround oases of water and gorgeous plantings. Cobblestone paths are warmed by the sun, and Adirondack chairs invite quiet reflection. The spa experience here is all about tactile sensation, and each guest is encouraged to move from areas of warmth to cold to relaxation as many times as he or she wants. The path could be a hot bath to an arctic waterfall to a hammock, or a sauna to a river swim to a seat by an outdoor fireplace. The idea is to both energize and relax the body, and all are done in silence—no talking in the steam room or solariums or anywhere else. Jolene and I made our way around the spa in many combinations, speaking only with nods and giggles. There was abundant time for being present and there were none of the typical distractions. Jolene should have been a stranger to me, but she was not. I felt as if I had always known her.

The next morning we commandeered one of the canopies the guys had brought to the racetrack and named it the Red Tent. Women gathered here and we shared food, stories, parenting woes, books of poetry, music, wisdom. They came because Jolene pulled them in. She welcomed each new visitor and brought her into the circle. It was as if each woman had been missing but now was found, as if the group was incomplete without her. It was what I imagine a women's retreat might be like, only this one sprang up effortlessly, buoyed by the irrepressible energy of a single person.

Jolene made it fun, certainly, but there was serious work going on as well. She had the ability to reach down into your core and pull something up you'd never seen before—a skill or gift you had, a dream you kept under wraps, an adventure you desperately wanted to take but were afraid to bring out into the open. She could tease this crystal out of anyone with love, and before they knew it they were talking about their most cherished desire. She was asking each of us, in the most gentle way, what our stand was—who we were and how we wanted to show up for this life.

She quickly dispensed with past baggage and present worries and told each of us we could be that person. But, if you pressed her on her methods, she would shake her head and laugh and say she was simply pointing out what was already in plain view.

I was my best self that weekend: open to friendships, sharing my experience, learning from those around me, and dancing with the present. In my mind, I often go back to that spa, to the red tent, to the connection with a sympathetic soul and know that something shifted in that weekend. I let go of some vision of myself that I was clinging to, someone who was just going to keep gliding through life, living with the guilt of not-writing and half-being. Instead, I made way for the me who would have to deal with real life as it lurked around the corner.

The Jolenes I have met are guides in my life. They reveal something new about myself, or give me faith that the path I am on is the right one. They show me the joy of sharing my experience of living, and I meet them in intense experiences that I can remember in detail. We converse at a level that is new to me, deeper and more meaningful than my day-to-day banter. Some of these friends I see every day and others at long intervals, but I always feel their impact like the hot-cold of the spa—startling, invigorating, and somehow rearranging my consciousness.

I see people differently now, because of these friend-guides, with far more compassion for them and me. I don't judge or compare as much as I once did. I don't make as many assumptions, and when I do, I check myself. I recognize people and situations that are harmful more clearly; I am not as easily snowed. I know that I do not know and cannot know the future, and worrying about it is pointless. But after this moment of crystallization, I also see what I will leave behind—the friendships that will become less significant. The triangle that our connection forms with the world will shrink, and this is painful. We will come to speak of unimportant things because we have grown apart, and I am sorry for this loss.

As I grieve for that lost friendship, a new one will appear. This person will speak the language I can now understand and is on a journey as well. For a time—a year, a decade, a lifetime—we will take the path together, forming a new shape for what friendship will be for each of us. We will cherish the lost friendships for the ways they made us grow and the gifts those friends and allies bestowed. Each of my friends has taught me how to be a person first, to get grounded before I seek new insight and new adventures, and for that I am forever grateful.

ON CHOICES
TREE POSE, VRKSASANA

Move from Triangle pose to Warrior II, then step your back foot forward and find Mountain Pose (Tadasana). Now shift all of your weight to your left leg. Feel that leg fire up from the ankle to the glutes. Feel yourself root into the ground. Firmly engage your abdominals. Hold your palms together in front of your heart, your fingers pointing straight up. This is an Anjali yoga mudra. Now bend your right knee and lift your right leg in front of you. Find your focused gaze, your drishti. Clear your

mind. Slowly turn your bent knee to the right and rest your right foot as high on your inner left leg as it will comfortably go. Press leg to foot and foot to leg, equal pressure. Keep both your hips facing forward. Stay perfectly balanced here, or gracefully raise your arms above you, like branches. Lift your gaze. Feel that you are a strong and beautiful tree, tied to the earth and also to the sun.

I often wonder if I found the house or if it found me. I had never noticed it before the "For Sale" sign went up, though I had passed it hundreds of times. Set back from the road, shaded by old trees, the little white farmhouse with the gracious front porch spoke to me. You belong here, it said, and I listened.

That night, I remember telling Carl that maybe the answer to our general discontent lay all around us. The floors we walked on, the roof that sheltered us, the walls that surrounded us were all part of an elaborate trap we had created. We had stumbled into this 3,200 square foot snare and had built a lifestyle that would necessitate it: two demanding jobs with two nice incomes, two children to be fed and clothed and doted upon, furnishings ample enough to fill the space.

Traps are ingenious devices. The best ones ambush you, plunging you into darkness as you step on a seemingly innocent pile of leaves. Because you are human, you make the best of the situation, determining how to protect yourself from the elements and fashioning sustenance from the materials at hand. Before you know it, you are making mud drawings on the walls, and the place feels like home.

So it is with the demands of society. We succumb to the trap of They. What will They think if we do or do not drive that car, live in that house, pursue that career? We worry that we may be shunned for not having as many things or not having enough to say for ourselves. We are afraid we might need to make excuses, and we are ashamed of this fear. Deep down, we know we are the designers of both our incarceration and our freedom. The key to our liberation is to remember what it is we want our life to be about. Without society's imagined judgments distracting our attention, the rope ladder is suddenly visible, and we can climb out.

The little farmhouse was my rope ladder. I clung to it and the vision of what our life would be like if we lived in it. It would necessarily be simpler, I determined. Two careers would no longer be needed; one whole or two halves would suffice. Lots of things would no longer be needed, so whole rooms of furniture and items we never used could go. We could pare it all down to only what was important to us: the big things like time for each other and our children, being connected to our community, and owning a piece of history; and the smaller things, like ancient trees and a perennial garden, a sunny woodworking shop, walking to school, and a porch swing. With all that we owned, we possessed none of these treasures.

Simplifying a life is not a simple process. It takes courage and what my grandmother would have called grit. It is unpleasant to face the mounds that collect in the basement over a decade or two. Everything must be touched. A thousand decisions must be made. Past attachment and future regret must be considered. Things cannot simply be tossed out, so homes must be found for the toys and the crib, the old computers, ragged beach chairs, clothes, appliances, scrap wood, and knickknacks. The pile you keep is whatever is essential—what will be needed and no more. A pile of Enough.

Grit will be essential as you explain yourself to others. People you love will admire and respect you for taking a stand and doing what you believe is right for you. They may not tell you this, but you will know. People you like will not always understand your decision, and they will say tactless things or bristle with discomfort. Some may think, erroneously, that you have passed judgment on their own lives. There will be some people in your life who do not make it into the pile of Enough.

Finally, the house you once loved needs to be left behind. When you first found each other, there was infatuation, then passion, and what should have grown into easy companionship. Like a hasty marriage gone sour, our love for our house had withered. Its imposing facade hid shoddy construction; it had no integrity. We had grown beyond it.

ON CHOICES

Choosing a new life was the easy part; we lived with our decision on moving day. I will long remember Carl's face as he stood in the tumbledown shed that would serve as his new garage, trying to fit three bays' worth of tools and equipment into that impossible space. With a snowfall threatening, it all became too much for him. "We made a mistake," he whispered, as we stood in the damp gloom, his face crumpled in pain and desperation. This was the frightening moment we had skirted in all the months of planning and purging, in the excitement of dreaming of what could be. I held that dream out to him again, reminded him of the new garage and woodworking studio soon to be built, reminded him of the big and small reasons for changing, and asked him to hold on.

From the distance of some years, I see that I was seeking not shelter but balance. My life had become one I could no longer justify to myself. My mother's sudden death had made me pay attention. The message I heard was "What if you die at 60, is this what you want to say for yourself? I was too busy to enjoy my children or my husband, or do anything I really loved to do, because I was working on becoming an executive." Leaving the corporate world was the first step I consciously took toward designing the life I wanted to live. Everything up to that point felt as if it was proscribed for me: good family, great education, exciting career, wonderful marriage, beautiful children. I was lucky; I came from a starting point that allowed me to carom along a track that would undoubtedly have made me satisfied. I had rolled to a stop, though. I thought there was something missing, and it was my responsibility to figure out what it was. Changing my environment—and taking on all the physical and mental and emotional upheaval it would require—was the next step.

At times I find myself gazing out at the road from the front porch, and I catch sight of my dog sleeping in the shade under the maple tree. We all love our little farmhouse with its quirks and strange angles, its history and charm, its layers of paint and the small treasures (glass bottles, old newspapers, the remnants of a shipping crate) it occasionally offers up. It is difficult to remember a life when there was no porch and no maple tree, when cars did not rumble by toward the town center, when different things were important. But I can recall that feeling of being torn between doubt and certainty. It was a courageous move, and it was jarring. It was like shifting all my weight to one side and trying to stand on one leg. Now I have brought the other leg to rest upon it and am raising my arms up in the air. I am writing my words on the sky. I am tied to the earth and also to the sun.

ON LOSS AND GRIEF
CHAIR POSE, UTKATASANA

After Tree Pose, stand in Mountain Pose. Bring both arms forward and raise them up above your head so your biceps are slightly in front of your face. Bend your knees and lower your hips as if you were sitting in a chair. Keep your torso as upright as possible and squeeze your inner thighs together. Hold this posture. Remember, it is simply sensation. Focus your mind on your drishti gaze. Breathe.

My yoga instructor says that the posture you dislike the most is the one that you most need to do. For many of us, it would have to be Chair Pose. So difficult to keep the torso upright while holding the arms overhead, so difficult to sit the hips down low while the quadriceps are screaming. So difficult to focus on the breath while the mind is adamantly begging you to stop the pain. You could do a whole yoga practice and avoid Utkatasana, but there would be this deceptively simple movement that you had never experienced. As painful as it is, it is part of yoga.

Losing someone you love is like the Utkatasana of life. You wish you did not have to experience it, but one day you do. There is pain that comes and goes, there is an ability to focus only on your grief and then to focus elsewhere for a time, there is the memory of the sensation even long after the event has passed. Death is natural, but it is deceptively cruel—your mind wants nothing to do with it, but your heart sits into it.

My mother died when she was 60, felled by a cerebral hemorrhage at the end of a beautiful May weekend. She had a brain tumor no one knew about, and she had probably had it for weeks or even months. We were the survivors: my dad, my brother and two sisters, our spouses, our children. We were stunned. After hearing from my father that my mother had collapsed, I left my house before dawn to drive the three hours to the hospital. I called my mother-in-law on the way just to hear her voice. I sobbed through those miles, begging for a miracle, knowing there would be none. At the hospital, my father and I had to make decisions about organ donation. I had to see my mother, a lifeless body filled with tubes. I remember calling my brother in Germany to tell him the news, telling him she was still on life support and we would wait until he could get there. I had to keep myself from sitting down and feeling the pain.

I picked up my sisters at the airport; I remember their faces crumpling on seeing me because being home made it real. We went to find a burial plot for our mother, walking the cemetery grounds and feeling so very lost. We chose a granite bench instead of a headstone and asked them to place it by the plum tree. We chose a coffin, we met with a minister, we met with a caterer, we answered the phone and the door, we held a funeral, we laid her to rest, we held a memorial service, we held an Irish wake. And then we started to grieve.

Grief is extraordinarily personal. I can only relate how I have navigated this strange country. The first few months were surreal. I went about my business as a mother and wife and employee and friend and let the fact of my mother dying sink in. She died so suddenly, that for weeks I would wake up and have to remind myself that she was gone. Each time it was a fresh grief, a cruel awakening to the new reality of my life: I no longer had a mother. Sometimes I would think someone on the street was Mom, and then as we passed I would see I was mistaken. I would be with other friends and their mothers and feel my loss keenly. I would calculate how many years I had lost with her—twenty or more?—and moan at how unfair life can be. I went to see a grief counselor who advised me to get really angry about my mother abandoning me; I found this advice absurd and never went back. Nine months after my mother died, I had a vivid dream about her. She was at a party, dressed beautifully and smiling broadly, dancing in the middle of the floor with light radiating all around her. "I'm okay," she mouthed. I woke up sobbing and knew that I had arrived in a new place. It was time to sit my heart right into grief and to feel it.

I thought about my mom a lot back then, realizing early how lucky I was to have her for 34 years. She was a natural and gifted teacher, still the smartest person I've ever known, fun-loving and curious, a strong feminist, an even stronger altruist, honest, kind, wise, gracious. She loved me very much, and she showed me every day. I started to feel sad about all that she had missed and would miss—grandchildren, her own children, her marriage, the plans they had made, world events, politics, travel. She died a week before her retirement party. She would miss growing old.

At first I lulled myself into thinking that because I was a grown woman, I would miss Mom's friendship but her work as a mother was done. Little did I know how much I could have used her advice and support as I raised two children, navigated a career, made sense of a school system, and learned the ropes of being a parent in a competitive town. I could have used my mother's practical sense of the world when situations felt confusing. I could have used her help in deciphering teenagers and grown women who acted like teenagers. My mother would have cooled my outrage at others' behavior and have asked me to examine my own culpability. She would have polished my rough edges with a gentle hand and helped me gain some wisdom. Instead, I learned the hard way how to handle a teacher's conference, how much to volunteer, what was expected from other parents to keep the playing field even, how to properly comfort a friend who was dying, how much humanity I could reasonably expect from a boss, when to say "no." I was far from complete when my mother died, and in many ways her real work was just beginning.

At five-year intervals we—my father, brother and two sisters—visit my mother's grave together. We gather from the east and west coasts and make a weekend of it. On Sunday, we sit in my dad's old beach chairs facing the rose quartz bench engraved with my mother's birth and death dates. We marvel at how the plum tree has grown. My father asks us to say a few words, if we want to. I find it hard to put into words the gravity of the situation in these moments, when my mother feels so close and also so far from the cemetery. There has been no glue to put us back together—that had been my mother's job. In the absence of that life force, it has become each of our own responsibilities. My father has remarried, a lucky man to find true love twice in his life. My brother has built a family and community of friends in the Midwest, and he is very content. My next younger sister landed on the West coast, having married just months before my mother's death, and is now the proud parent of two energetic grade schoolers. My youngest sister has perhaps struggled most with this loss and has reminded me that we must grieve both the dark and light side of the person we loved.

To be sure, my mother was a person with flaws and baggage like all of us. She never shared stories of her childhood with us in all the years I knew her; in fact, it was after her funeral that my aunt told us what it was like to be raised by two heavy drinkers who loved their children, but were also distracted by their habit. It was typical that my grandmother would take her three daughters to pick up my grandfather at the end of a working day and make a family stop at the bar near the train station. My mother refused to leave the car and join them; she was 8 years old when she made the fierce decision to have nothing to do with the lifestyle they were offering. This meant an adulthood of reinvention and a bit of hiding. She was overly concerned with being appropriate at all times, keeping up the façade, and avoiding the judgment of others. Her deepest disappointments with her own children came when we crossed these lines and made her "look bad." Her first impulse in many new situations was to hang back a bit, even though her intellect and charm would have carried her easily through any situation. Late in life she fully recognized her own essential worthiness, so busy was she for 60 years trying to make sure that every bit of armor around her—children, marriage, home, career—was polished to an unassailable shine. I believe she knew this about herself and could see her self-imposed limitations clearly. Her ardent hope for her children was that we transcend them in our own lives.

Each person we love and lose leaves behind the gifts of their existence. If we are to move beyond grief, we must come to understand those gifts. They become the talismans on our journey; they light our way. My mother gave me intelligence and curiosity. She showed me resilience, rebuilding her life after a dysfunctional childhood and acting with class and grace in every aspect of her existence. She gave me a model for mothering, showing affection through words and deeds, allowing her children to become independent. She practiced a life of service to others and showed us that this provided one with deep contentment. She challenged the conventional thinking of the world, asking others to defend their beliefs and to investigate their underpinnings. She wrote essays and poetry, posting the poems on the refrigerator for our perusal and critique. She read as a hobby, and she read voraciously. She gave me books, pressing them upon me, leaving them draped around me throughout our home, filling every bookcase to bursting with every kind of written word. She was fiercely loyal to her many students, pushing them to grow, to be better, to never take the easy way out in thinking or in writing. She showed me delight when I did something really well; she showed me dark days of disappointment when I lied to her or gave up on myself. She gave me the freedom to be myself by never criticizing; she had faith in me. Because of my mother, I have compassion for myself when I make a mistake, I have strength to withstand the blows that inevitably mark a lifetime, and I have love to give and receive that fills me up and makes me whole.

I honor my mother by letting these gifts, her light, shine in my life, disbursing the shadows and opening myself up to the mystery and joy. She would say that every day is a miracle and a wonder, a moment to become more fully ourselves. This is sitting into life, this is Utkatasana: a little painful, full of intent, requiring great strength and a willingness to be vulnerable—a beautiful expression of what it is to be human and what it is to be loved.

ON FAIRNESS
CROW POSE, BAKASANA

Bend forward in Chair Pose and place your hands about one foot ahead of your feet on the mat. Bend your knees deeply, and bend your elbows. Lean forward so that your knees rest on your triceps. Look forward as you tighten your abdominals. Your gaze will pull your center of gravity forward and your feet will rise off the mat. You are suspended, holding your weight on your hands. You are a bundle of beak and wings on tiny "feet". You are a crow, a rook, a raven.

The first time I saw someone do Crow, I was stunned. I thought of yoga as mat work, whereby either your four limbs were firmly planted on the ground, or one or both your legs were holding the rest of you upright. The idea of suspending myself on my hands seemed impossible. I tried to just force myself into the pose, as if by sheer will I would make it happen. I'd heave myself up but my legs would stay earthbound or I'd fall over on my side or I'd pull back just as it got scary. In the meantime, I went about the business of learning the other postures and focusing on control and balance. I decided Crow was not for me. Then it happened: I stopped thinking about the instructions—bent elbows, knees on triceps, head looking forward, abdominals tight—and felt the fluid motion of Crow. Rather than make myself get there, I had arrived.

The more you learn in yoga, the more you realize how much there is to learn. Just as I conquer Bakasana, I understand that there is far more depth to it. From my tucked up position, I see that I could make myself more upright, that my abdominals could fire more strongly, and that I could work to find my drishti gaze. I could smile. Now that I have imitated a Crow, I could become one.

Hindus believe that when a crow shows up at your doorstep, he is carrying information for you about your situation. Crows are considered advanced communicators, as they signal each other with unique and distinctive calls. The crow is one of the most intelligent of all animals, both an indiscriminate scavenger and a user of innovative tools. They are quite social, but I think of them as studious birds. They survey, they consider, they pause. As I pause in Bakasana, I wonder what the Crow is in my own life. That is, what is the posture that has eluded me, or the new perspective I can bring to my own situation of living and being human. First, I must get clear on how I have been shaped to think and feel the way I do and the lessons I may have missed along the way.

I was raised by a feminist and a chauvinist, two would-be social reformers in a world of elite privilege. Both were liberals, brought up by middle class parents in New York City. My parents got along famously, and they agreed on almost every element of childrearing. Their core value was education, and they moved to Greenwich, Connecticut, a wealthy suburb of New York City with outstanding public schools, when the first two of their four children were toddlers. They left the middle class behind as my father joined a Fortune 500 company on the management track. My mother left her teaching career behind to focus on full-time motherhood.

Their campaign to open our eyes to the real world started early and boldly. My parents brought all four of us, aged 4, 6, 8, and 10, to Harlem to spend a Saturday clearing a vacant lot. We worked with the neighbors and shoveled debris, painted the walls, and installed playground equipment. Not only was the work different from our regular chores, but the place was strikingly different: treeless, tall cement buildings surrounding soulless courtyards, and vacant lots full of trash and graffiti. We were out of our element, but unafraid. At the end of the day, we all joined together for dinner at a long, communal table in the middle of the street. I remember bright colors and lots of laughter, delicious smells and a feeling of happiness. I started that morning knowing everything about my world and ended it knowing that I had much to learn. I'm sure my parents were proud of all of us, but that day did not get mentioned much in the ensuing years. It became part of the fabric of our family, just one thread among multitudes.

There ensued many more visits to Harlem, as we had four Fresh Air Fund kids visit us over four or five consecutive summers. Frankie, Sheila, Carla, and Otelia spent two weeks with us going to the beach and getting ice cream, riding our bikes and playing endless games of tag. It was such fun to have another sister my same age, and it was wild to have eight kids in the house. We so far outnumbered the adults that any fragile balance of power was gone. We put on plays for my parents and went on field trips to museums and took ferry rides on Long Island Sound. At the end of the two weeks, we brought each of them home to an apartment that was a stark contrast to our sprawling colonial. We met their single mothers and their siblings who stayed behind. My mother—who did most of the planning and driving and care and feeding over these two weeks—did not instruct us on how to act in this new situation; she just drove us to the Projects, crammed us into the creaky elevators, and said hello to anyone we met in the hallways. She laughed and joked with the women who had entrusted her with their children in the same way she laughed with her own friends. She taught us, without ever saying the words, that we are all just people, some good, some wonderful, some not, who are living the best we can in the lives we have.

It was my father who taught her—as he taught us—these ways of being. Dad could and did talk to anyone. Train conductors, schoolteachers, celebrities, bus boys, politicians, porters, executives, people standing ahead of him in line, people waiting to cross a street—each of them was someone he was curious about. He went beyond pleasantries with these strangers, asking about their jobs and their lives. His impulse was so subconscious that he would often assume the accent of the person to whom he was speaking. It would have seemed insulting if his interest in them had not been so genuine. In an elevator ride, he could effortlessly extract genders and ages of children, hometowns, and professions of the fellow riders. A tour bus was a smorgasbord of opportunity for him to make connections. Because he was sincerely interested, people liked him. He was, and still is, a collector and keeper of stories. Of course, as teenagers we found all of this interaction painfully embarrassing. But before and after those awkward years, we were proud of my father's ability to be an every man. He would cast off the trappings of race and class as if they were useless burdens, and he would delight in being free of them.

We understood in those Fresh Air summers that some of us had far more choices than others, for no other reason than our skin was white. One hot day Sheila and I rode our bikes over to our swim club. This was the family hangout all summer, a relaxed and no frills swim and sailing club very different from the golf and tennis clubs dotted all over town. We kids would spend whole summer days there, taking sailing lessons, swimming in the pool, playing card games in the snack bar, and treating ourselves to ice cream on account. No parents were needed, as there were lifeguards and sailing and swim coaches and a bevy of old ladies who watched over the place from their beach chairs. We never got away with anything, so we just went about the business of being part of a summer social life. Kids had odd nicknames, extended families of cousins ruled the place, and the best swimmers and divers were like royalty. We had freedom, and we had a little swagger.

I was excited to share this world with Sheila, but as I nonchalantly signed her in as my guest, there was some hesitation on the part of the gatekeeper. He grudgingly let us in, and I shrugged it off as general adult crankiness. As we moved around the pools and picnic tables, though, I felt the stares and the hushed tones of others. Sheila being black was suddenly of note, and we were being politely shunned. It felt strange and wrong and confusing. After a while,

Sheila tugged my arm and said we should probably leave. I was ashamed about our ill treatment, but was not sure how to apologize. Sheila said it happened all the time and it was no big deal.

I look back now and wonder at my parents' motivations. They must have believed so strongly in giving other children an opportunity, that they ignored the judgment of their friends and even risked losing them. They knew we kids would also be snared by these rules, but they let us feel their sting. A year or two after that incident, my parents recommended close friends for the swim club. The board rejected the family on grounds that they had brought African-American children into their home. We agreed as a family to withdraw from the club. I spent my teen summers at the beach, the gathering place for the town that did not seem to have a color code.

It is always "a big deal" to discriminate, that was the lesson of my childhood. Growing up in one of the whitest, most affluent and most conservative towns in America, it was a lesson that had to be shown and felt—it was not an academic exercise. It would have been simple to take us all away to some secluded lake house instead of insisting that our friends be part of our world in every way. It would have been understandable, and far more acceptable to others, to teach us that privilege was our birthright and that we need only move forward from that place. We had to see that friendship was easy but that rules and reasons sometimes made it complicated.

This was the genius of my parents, believing that we needed to have opportunities to grow just as much as the so-called underprivileged children who lived a train ride and a world away. They knew the core must be strong in order to dispel fear and say and do the courageous thing. They wanted us to be able to survey, to consider, and to pause—to decide for ourselves. They wanted us to be crows in our own lives.

ON EQUALITY
BRIDGE POSE, SETU BANDHASANA

From Crow pose, thrust your legs backward and into Plank. Lower yourself to the floor and roll over on your back. Bend both knees and place your feet on the floor, hip distance apart and parallel. Place your hands by your sides and make sure you can just brush the back of each heel with your longest fingertips. Contract your abdominal muscles and push through your heels to raise your thighs, buttocks, and back off the ground. Squeeze your shoulder blades together, and clasp your hands together underneath you, pressing your arms along the mat. Push your chest toward your chin while your head rests on the mat. You are the bridge between the past and the future, the bridge of the present time.

In the late 1960s, women's consciousness was being raised across the country. The gains women had made in the job force during World War II had withered in the 1950s, as an era of ease and convenience swept across America. Ease meant the husband could work and the wife would stay home and care for the children in a pretty house, with a nice car, and with all the modern conveniences. As 1970 approached, many women were finding out this was not their dream.

In my leafy East Coast suburb, my mother and her friends were thrilled to be part of a movement that their generation started. My mother believed that equality across all lines—gender, race, religion, sexual orientation—was a fundamental right, that it came with being human. It was perhaps her organizing principle, the one thing about her that never changed, that she would defend, and that she would call you on if she caught you thinking differently. She may have thought it both ludicrous and exciting that women's equality was to become part of the constitution—ludicrous because it was so obvious, and exciting because it would be the law. She brought me to New York City in August of 1970 to join the ERA march up Fifth Avenue. I was eight years old and my memories are hazy, but I do remember her excitement and pride in being a part of history as we took the train to Grand Central Station and joined the thousands of marchers. There were women of all ages carrying signs and singing songs. I remember holding Mom's hand and feeling that this day was about joy.

There was so much hope for women balancing the world back then, but something happened to the trusses in the 30 years between that joyful march and the new millennium. We are all familiar with the startling statistics that although women are 50% of the population, they hold relatively few positions of influence in business and politics. We know that the Equal Rights Amendment was never ratified. We know that violence against women is on the rise, and that whole countries of women are kept under wraps. We know that in some parts of the world girls are not educated, although their brothers are. We know this is not because women are not capable. In fact, women have proven to have the same capacity as their male counterparts to do the jobs that need to be done. Those of us in the first generation of women to have the choice to take any job we wanted, or to stay home, lost our footing. We were ready to change the world, but it was not ready to be changed.

My father told me I should be a teacher, that the rough-and-tumble world of business was not for me. For all his belief in opportunities, my father could never quite see a woman being equal to a man in business. He was certainly proud of me, but there was a sub-theme of taking my rightful place as wife and mother that still comes through today. I understand him as a man of his generation, and he comes by his chauvinism honestly. My mother worked hard throughout her marriage to point out the error of his logic, but in the world he moved in he saw a different reality.

Being my mother's daughter, I went into business anyway. When I got there I found men (and women) just like my father, who did not quite know what to do with what I brought to the table. I was too curious and too clear about what needed to change. I understood the corporate system, could see its cracks and flaws, and I thought it best to point them out. Since I understood the workings of the infrastructure, I believed that improving them would improve all the lives within it. While that may be true, if we change the system, we also impact individuals who do not want to lose power, money, or status. This was the chasm I kept coming up to just before I had to give up and move on to the next situation.

I was an enigma to many of my employers: capable of creating solid work product, not very interested in pushing my own agenda, and easy to take advantage of. I gave away my power every day in the form of good ideas that others took credit for. Because I so fiercely wanted to do the very thing I was told I could not—be successful in business—I changed myself. I toed the line, dressed the part, didn't rock the boat, was the company man. I was a woman who showed up at work but was not actually there. I learned how to do just what was expected, maybe a little more, and to do it within the parameters that would be accepted. Eventually, I stopped sharing my good ideas altogether. I did not respect most of the people I worked for and learned that was normal and acceptable. My titles and salary claimed I was successful, but just as I attained them I realized they were ill-gotten gains. If you lose your integrity in the pursuit of your dream, your dream is the wrong one.

For me, becoming an independent consultant was a bid for freedom. I would decide my own rules, my fees, my methodology, and my choice of projects. I would be able to speak truth to power because I was getting paid to do so, and to provide any less to my clients would be a disservice. I would not be harassed or ignored, and I would be respected for my way of seeing. I would have to give up the chance to directly lead people and organizations, but I knew I could grow as a leader in other ways. The choice I made has been good for me personally, but, still, I am more of an architect than a hands-on corporate bridge-builder.

I now see women crossing the same spans I found challenging. Increasingly, women are showing up and standing in their power. Perhaps we have said "enough!" or we no longer care to define ourselves in relationship to men. I see women taking their place in sports, business, the arts, politics, communications, and not simply doing it as men do it but defining how women do it. A woman takes the pole position at a NASCAR race and is asked about her boyfriend and fellow driver. If she cares, she hardly shows it. She has legions of fans who adore her for who she is— smart, beautiful, talented. She flaunts her sexuality along with her driving skill, a signal to the rest of us that she is a complete person. A woman serves as the United States Secretary of State for four years and is asked about her clothing designer. If she is offended, she brushes it off with a quip. Her work over those deadly and complicated years is impressive—relentless, practical, tough-minded—and is a reflection of her own personality. Six actresses in serious films are included in a campy send-up on Oscar night that minimizes their work down to the fact that they showed their breasts in each film. If they are insulted, they do not break character and their faces never belie their emotions. They know their work is unassailable, including the breast baring.

I am always surprised that there is a commotion made around each of these women—still—for being a woman and doing the job. They are all experts at their craft and role. They have earned their place, working hard to maintain a sense of self in a world that might have other ideas for them. They do not make excuses, and they do not expect perfection. They are putting their gifts to work every day.

It seems simple enough. But, the world I live in, the one where most of us reside, is one where we argue openly about the choices women make about their bodies. Not everyone can agree on whether rape is rape or if no means no. When a new book about how women can choose to make their way to the highest levels of corporate America was published to great fanfare, news stories rehashed the debate about working and non-working mothers. We are still celebrating women's history month, as if half of the population was a special class worthy of an annual award. We are easily distracted from the basic fact of our necessity to the world, our attention pulled into controversies that should have been laid to rest long ago.

Across the socioeconomic spectrum, across jobs, throughout academia, across every method of delivering us entertainment and information, there is a belief among many people that women should be treated as different, or less than. The truth is, women and men are equal and are entitled to the same unalienable rights. They are not two different species, one is not superior to the other, one does not legislate for the other, one is not the property of the other, and one is not an object while the other is a subject. This is a difficult concept for many men and women to accept; it upsets the status quo and threatens a loss of power or status or order. The potential gain, though, is worthy of consideration: once it is set free, our feminine power could arrest the carnage that is the accepted condition of living in a masculine world. Equality is the keystone that will keep our world from crumbling.

There are recent signs of bridge building, despite those who would prefer to keep the genders divided. Violence against women is increasing, but we are hearing about it more as well. Women are speaking out, and people are learning to place blame where it belongs, on the perpetrator not the victim. In some arenas, gender is becoming less important as a differentiator. In sports in particular, fans today can be awed by speed and endurance in any body, male or female. We are delving into the reasons women are not succeeding in certain fields, and why girls are not being educated, and working to remove specious obstructions. In the 1970s we marched on Washington, now many of us are marching across the Internet, posting our thoughts in blogs and tweets and videos as they occur to us. We don't need to organize. We are one, loud voice proclaiming that the culture that objectifies or demeans women is wrong. This is a seismic shift. You cannot quiet all the voices, and when the voices are 50 percent of the population, you might as well just sit back and listen. In listening to each other, we will divine the truth.

There is a great chasm between women and men, and we see it more clearly now than we did a generation ago. Across this distance we make disastrous assumptions about each other, we alienate one another, and we turn our backs to one another. Some of us fall into the abyss, their lives ruined by the violence and the violations. The only way to heal the world is to take what is best about us, the best of the masculine and the feminine, and apply it to solving what ails all of us: poverty, violence, oppression, illness, vice. We must find a way to cross the chasm. We will need to start with abutments that carry the load as we arch across the span toward each other. I will lay some stones with my words, someone else will speak, someone else will teach, someone else will sing, someone else will parent, someone else will simply be herself. Each of us can use the foundations we have within us to build the bridge of the present time.

ON SPIRITUALITY
WHEEL POSE, URDHVA DHANURASANA

From Bridge pose, place your hands by your ears, palms on the floor and fingers pointing toward your feet. Press down so that the crown of your head is on the floor. Now, push up through your arms and thighs, keeping your abdominals taut, and raise your back higher off the floor. You are in a backbend with hands and feet supporting you. You are a semicircle, an arc, a crescent, a dome. You are your own temple, containing all the treasures of the universe.

It is unexpected to approach Saint Paul's Cathedral from the side, the churchyard. As I step through the gate, I feel the whisper of calm and peace that I increasingly feel when I am in the presence of spirituality. The garden of crisscrossing paths and statues is lovely, hinting at the grandeur around the corner, but virtually empty. This is not the thing to see, but it captures the intended spirit: calm strength, hope, peace, grace.

The proper entrance to the cathedral is grand, for certain, and a testament both to the men who built it and their determination to reflect the glory of their god. Inside, it is God's greatness in man's image, crafted from stone and wood, granite and glass. The arches beneath the dome are impossibly high, the stonework beyond compare, the length and breadth exceeding every expectation. People wander and gaze, some pray and light votives. I am at once awestruck and ambivalent. I cannot feel a warm presence in those cold stones, and I am disappointed. I understand the need to express, to testify, but I wonder what is lost. For that temple, made to stand forever, is empty of feeling and full of things.

I am trying to build my own cathedral. Progress is slow. I have struggled with the architecture and the interiors. I have scrapped some plans. Over a lifetime, though, I have shaped my own faith and spirituality and they give me a foundation and, at unexpected moments, wings.

As a young girl made to attend Mass at the Catholic Church, I found religion strange and mysterious. The priest wore robes, bells were rung, incense burned. There were solid gold plates, colored windows, a man hanging on a cross. We sat and then we stood, sometimes we kneeled. We said the words we were instructed to say. We listened to the stories of the Bible and the lessons hidden within them. Mass had a beginning and an end and the same activities throughout. There were pageants and palms and communion dresses and confessions. The events of the year, the events of a Mass, they both lulled me and made me restless.

My family's church was a hive of activity, and my mother was perennially involved with its good works. We held a rummage sale every year to which my father's company provided many of the prizes. The annual father-daughter dance was held in the church hall. There was a telephone chain and meals to bring to those suffering loss. There were collections taken for those in need. These were practical things, and I understood them.

Religious education meant Wednesday afternoons at the Convent of the Sacred Heart, a trip of 30 minutes from school with my best friend and co-conspirator. Mary and I munched on Mallomar cookies in the backseat of her station wagon, listening to Oldies 108, resigned to this particular obligation. Buzzed on sugar and Motown, we learned from the convent sisters the tenets of Catholicism, the meaning of the sacraments, the requirements of our chosen religion. We learned that gray-haired men could dispense the communion wafers and that our favorite nun could play the guitar. We wrote Bible verses in thick notebooks and practiced drinking wine from a chalice. As we grew older, we discussed the underpinnings of what it was to be a good Catholic, what was expected of us, and how we were to live our lives.

Although I asked, no catechism teacher could explain to me why nuns could never be priests and why non-Catholics were doomed to an eternity in hell. Not one could prove to me that it was God for certain who created the world, this world, the one where girls were not as good as boys and other people were not as good as my fellow church goers. Those things, I was told by the men in the robes, were to be taken on faith. I spent my Sundays staring at the man on the cross and was not sure I cared anymore about the mystery. I was 13.

I left the Catholic Church the day after my confirmation. My concession to my mother was that I would be confirmed so that I could get another sacrament under my belt and, therefore, to hedge my bets. My concession to my grandmother was that I would be married in the Catholic Church; I fulfilled her wish 10 years later, but the obligation was to her, not to the sacraments.

Freedom from religion is a condition all its own. You have made the choice to be cast out of the cathedral; you do not want them, and they do not want you. The very foundations upon which you were building have been lost to you. In fact, the architecture itself has been lost to you. You must find your own beliefs, your own system for scaffolding your soul.

As a young mother, I thought it important that my children be christened (one Episcopal, one Unitarian) and that they have religious instruction (Congregationalist). It didn't take. My daughters fought going to church as I had. They didn't like the clothes they had to wear, the hard pews, the teachers, the Bible crafts. Even without a crucifix in sight, they found the atmosphere stifling. I was without the means to make them stay. Despite the transporting choir music and the peace I found sitting in the lovely white chapel, it was too difficult to make church-for-others a matter of principle.

For a time I went to the white chapel on my own, still seeking. I thought about my upbringing with the Angry God and his Suffering Son. I let the words and the music wash over me. I considered that there must be more to this world than mere chance and chaos, but that a god that fits into a book or the boundaries of a cathedral or set of requirements did not fit the grandeur of the universe. By defining God one way, I limited that god's reach. The world is full of mysteries that tap the ancient core of us, that make us look inside ourselves and consider not only *who* God is but *where* God is. How do we explain symphonic music, the way the sight of the ocean or a vast canyon makes you feel, poetry, the kindness of strangers, or beauty? How do we explain love? I believe that God is love: the love we have inside ourselves, the love we share, that love that causes us pain and joy to such an extent that we believe we may blow apart. Once I knew this, I walked out of the chapel and never returned. I had laid the cornerstone.

Not long ago, an acquaintance asked me which church I attended. When I responded that I didn't attend church, she blithely said, "oh, you're an atheist." No, I thought, I do believe, but a ready-made church was not able to solve my need for spiritual blueprints. I have been conscious for a long time that I am connected within the universe. I feel things deeply, I observe, I listen for the messages wrapped in coincidences and chance meetings. I believe we choose our lives and also that fate happens to us. I believe we are each on a journey and meant to learn and grow through every trial and joy. I believe the god we seek is the love and compassion inside each one of us, and that this connects us, and that it is deeply spiritual.

My spiritual explorations give shape and form to my cathedral. When I am open to the lessons, I find I am infused with understanding far beyond mere tenets and ancient words.

The sand mandala is in a temple, a makeshift one within a black box theatre. The ebony walls create the backdrop for saffron curtains and bright portraits of Hindu gods. The altar is capped by a framed photograph of the Dalai Lama, and arrayed beneath it are offerings: apples, flowers, butter sculptures, artwork made from sand. The sacred sand painting is created on a flat platform about three feet off the floor. The nuns, robed in maroon, sit quietly on the platform, hunched over as they rub silver sticks together to eke out the sand into the intricate design.

People mill about, watching the nuns at their work. No one speaks in more than a whisper. My friend, Donna, and I are completely rapt, forgetting time and place as we watch the final pieces of the design take on form and color. The feeling in the room is one of peace, like my heart is gently being massaged to work out the hurt and anger so that I can open it to the world.

The mandala itself, a wheel of color and shape representing the world and the human spirit at once, is dazzling. The Hindu nuns work painstakingly for 30 days on their ancient offering, knowing it will be destroyed on the 31st day. They follow the design, they meditate, they eat and sleep and pray. That is all they do and it is enough. It is a testament to hard work, painstaking care, creativity, joy, acceptance, and being. It will last the month and then the sand will be swept into jars and tossed into the river.

The mandala teaches a profound lesson about loss and what is left behind. I want to keep something tangible of that impermanent temple—a little bit of sand, maybe—to buttress my own, but it is not to be. Instead, it takes a place in my heart and mind, and makes me reflect on the cathedrals we build and the ones we find, the ones we cannot touch and the ones we live within. This is the final lesson of cathedrals: they take the shape and form of our souls, they are as broad and deep as we are, and they will never be completed because we will never be completed. And so I excavate the site, I shape the foundation and capture the scale, and I build the arches to graze the sky.

ON LOVE
COW FACE POSE, GOMUKHASANA

Lower yourself from Wheel pose gently to lie on your back. Roll over to your stomach and push up into Down Dog. Bring one leg forward, between your hands, then tuck the other behind it. Sit on the mat with both knees bent, one stacked on top of the other. Your buttocks should be firmly on the mat, and your feet, now on either side of you, should be equidistant from your hips. Sit up tall, then lean forward with a straight back, and place your hands on the mat in front of you. Perhaps you can rest your chin on your knee. Relax, breathe. You are self-contained, at peace with the world, quiet, gentle. You are complete as you are.

I am happiest in Gomukhasana. This is the only pose I can do completely and effortlessly. It is as if my body was made for this wrapping around itself. In this pose I can breathe, I do not think, I can be eternally present. It is a pose of deep comfort and contentment. I do not analyze it, and I do not care how anyone else experiences it. It is as if it is my own pose, created just for me. I am whole. It feels a lot like love.

I am married to the best friend I have ever known. We met when we were just kids, teenagers in a high school biology class. My friend Steve and I shared a lab table with Carl and his friend, Dave. The three guys were stocked with a dry wit, and I was the perfect straight man. Class was fun because I knew I would laugh. I never really noticed the rest of the class, intent as I was on keeping track of the jokes as they swept around the lab table. Steve was an old friend, Dave was a brilliant iconoclast, and Carl was a mystery. He was fun yet reserved, and I sensed depths there. I was young, though, and not very confident. I did not see it as my place to start the conversation.

Carl made the first move, asking me on a date one December Friday as he followed me back to my locker. I stalled for time and asked him to call me the next day. When he called he offered three options for the date: dinner, a movie, or ice skating. Dinner seemed like too much of an investment, and a movie theatre was no place to have a conversation, so I opted for ice skating. Carl picked me up in his VW

Beetle and we drove to the rink across town, the place most of us had learned to skate. I had been here often, of late, watching intramural hockey games with my friends. One day in the stands my crush at that time had even pointed out Carl in his hockey gear and told me he was the one for me. I brushed it off as nonsense, as we all do any time a love interest broadly hints that we are not the one for him.

We skated for a while, me stumbling about with my two or three moves and Carl gracefully sliding across the ice, backwards, forwards, around me, beside me. When we stopped, we sat on the bleachers in our skates, talking about our families and friends and the things that were important at 16. That conversation was the beginning of us: listening, sharing, dreaming, laughing. When we have run into the tough times as parents and as people, I have always known that at the heart of us is that ongoing conversation and the clear-eyed view of each other and the love, the deep, deep love for each other just as we are.

When the rink closed, we wanted to keep talking so we went to Dairy Queen for an ice cream. We were alone except for a young man lazily sweeping the place. At one point I looked over at the bored sweeper and realized he was the first boy who had ever asked me out, a handsome kid with a bad boy reputation. I had shut the door on that relationship after five days, because I knew he was all wrong for me. On that night, the universe presented me with a stark contrast, and I paid attention: this was no ordinary date, Carl was no ordinary boy.

The story from there is a familiar one. We fell in love, we went to college, we broke up, we got back together, we got our first jobs, we got married. In a few years, we had a house and two children, two careers, two extended families, friends, hobbies, plans. We made huge decisions together and supported each other through the inevitable ups and downs. There has been loss in both our families, there have been trials with our children, there have been career fits and starts. Life is not easy, but it is much easier if within it there is a place of comfort, a place to be wrapped up and safe.

I find it fascinating that how-to books are written about marriage. The lifetime commitment of two souls to each other cannot be put into a process or described as universal dos and don'ts. A marriage is not something to be imitated or replicated. A marriage is a complex organism, and essentially a fragile one. In the crash of a marriage ending, like the crashing of a plane, the possessions will survive intact, but the people will not. They are too fragile. This is why marriage is work—it requires attention and maintenance and care, every day, without fail. That work is very personal to the relationship, though, and there is no universal set of tools. The only thing that could usefully be written about marriage is the story of each one, and even then parts will be left out. A marriage is the same story told by two different people, simultaneously.

Who Carl is, he is to me. I can describe him by what he does, but that is not him. He is intelligence and humor and kindness and stubbornness and adventure. He is about being useful in his time here, always doing, always producing. He has high expectations for his fellow travelers because he believes we can all be doing more. He can fix anything, and if the solution is not obvious he will find one and make it work. He is fiercely protective of the people he loves, and he is not afraid to feel pain for them. He is brave and he is vulnerable and he is comfortable with both. He is so very kind to me, both when I am at my best and at my worst. He never loses faith in me or us. Best of all, Carl is still a mystery, with depths to discover. We are the combination of each of our selves and the amalgam of us-ness created by that coming together. We are the love that comes from being willing to grow another person and to be grown by him in turn.

I care for our love as if it is a living thing. It has its own energy and takes up space. It needs to be fed and sheltered. This is the work of marriage, the conscious creating of love. It comes from giving time and attention because the person you love needs it, listening beyond the words spoken, voicing your convictions, being honest, being patient, believing in the other person, having faith, letting go of control. It comes from caring about whatever the person you love cares about. I might have spent most of my adult life reading instead of getting off the rim and pitching a tent, learning about light and shadow and composition, riding my bicycle for ice cream, or counting turtles on the riverbank from my kayak, if not for Carl. I am fairly certain I would never have learned to bleed the brakes of a car, assisted in gluing up woodworking joints, or rebuilt a front porch from the studs. Offering and accepting the invitation to share each other's worlds is what makes each of us a whole person. Loving like this is the most important work I have ever done and the reason for every good thing in my life.

In our hearts we are 16 still, young and free and sweet, alive to the possibilities of our dreams. Each day we continue the grown up conversation, asking for advice and giving it, sharing opinions and defending them, remarking at our similar view of events and people. Our commitment as children to grow each other into adults is unique. I know this now. Perhaps that is why, no matter which words we use to tell it, our story feels like Gomukhasana: self-contained, created together, kind and loving, intimate and joyful, demanding only that we bring our best selves to it. It is at once complete, yet complete only for the present; it is changing but so subtly that the world cannot see it. It is two souls independent and intertwined, two lives, one story.

ON WRITING
PIGEON POSE, EKA PADA RAJAKAPOTASANA

Sitting upright in Cow Face pose, lean forward and place your hands on the floor in front of you. Move your legs back and find Down Dog. Raise one leg up behind you and bend that knee. Bring the leg forward so that the bent knee is resting on the ground, your shin is (eventually) parallel to the front of your mat, and your other leg is flat on the mat, pointing behind you. Hold yourself upright for a few breaths, and then surrender into the pose: bring your torso toward the mat and stretch your arms in front of you. This pose is a strong hip opener and deceptively

difficult to hold for a long time. You are building your inner and outer strength and opening yourself to meet your muse.

More than two years have passed since I began writing this book. When I started it, I thought of it as a four- or five-page essay that would cover about a dozen yoga poses in a lighthearted way. I would offer a minute glimpse into my inner world, and my reader would have to be satisfied with that. I knew I was capable of stringing words together and telling a short story, and I believed that was what I was called to do.

As my intrepid writing partner, Carolyn, read each snippet and pushed me to expand my offering, the work began to mean more to me than an experiment in the craft of writing. It was not only that I had opinions or observations to share with others, but that writing had things to teach me about me. The things I learned were alternately painful, stunning, embarrassing, and exhilarating. At times I wanted to walk away, but I pressed on if only because I was curious as to how the story would turn out.

The Mandala Writers Circle, a writing group that Carolyn and I created as an act of both inspiration and desperation, is the reason I completed this book. Our weekly meetings allowed us to share our beliefs on the page and with each other, without judgment and without criticism. We asked only that we each make our meaning clear to the reader. Our conversations about writing turned into a blog and website because we wanted to share with other fledgling writers (and others fighting their own artistic cobras) the tips and insights we had gained in approaching writing as a team sport. That endeavor—also momentous for us—allowed us to dream audaciously, to make serendipitous connections, and to sit with the reality of being a writer every day.

I have no writing regimen because I have never been good at disciplined living. I can write on paper or on a machine the same way I can read on paper or on a machine: words are words, stories are stories. The trouble has come in trying to reconcile the instructions from other writers that one must write every day with the reality that I don't always make it to the writing chair. After berating myself about this for months, I recognized that I write in my head between writing "sessions," or in what I affectionately call The Gap. In fact, I write in almost all of my waking moments. I write in the shower, I write while running errands, I write when I should be listening to my loved ones, I write in elevators. I am writing as I wake up each morning, writing out of my dreams. In fact, much of what I always understood as thinking was really forming words around those thoughts, exploring how I might present them to someone else. Writing for me has become a conscious effort to attend more closely to those thoughts, to mind the gap. That is, to capture the filament of an idea, and to let it spin outward, finding its own course. It is not a hunt for perfection but a search for meaning.

With me on the platform of creating are two companions, faith and memory. It takes a strong belief in one's thought-forming ability to allow the words to charge and sputter, and an even stronger faith to believe I will remember those wayward thoughts. When I feel the words slipping away, I sit down to put them on paper. In this act of commitment, they become real. They never seem quite as transporting as they were in my mind, but in writing them down, I learn where the words and I were going, and often the destination surprises me.

The act of writing used to seem mysterious, but now it is as concrete as any other endeavor. You cannot get better at it unless you do it, and you cannot do it unless you know you can always get better at it. The real mystery of writing, then, is not the doing of it, but the changes it engenders. Every time I write, I walk away from the task a different person. The things you write become part of you as, paradoxically, you let them go out into the world.

I think about Harper Lee, diligently setting down *To Kill A Mockingbird*, keeping the tone loving and the words spare. I wonder if she was consciously creating or if she was simply compelled to tell the story, her story. I imagine Reynolds Price sitting and conducting the light and energy to bring forth *Kate Vaiden* and to imprint upon us a place and time as much as a character. I am awestruck at how Robertson Davies imagined worlds within worlds that would fit inside his head, or how Isabel Allende is able to cast a spell and stop the reader in her tracks, or how E. B. White can make me laugh and cry and shake my head at his extraordinary use of words in *One Man's Meat*. Jane Austen gave us clever social insight and Ruth Oseki gave us metaphysics, as gifts. These writers, and legions of others, are able to go beyond telling a tale and add layer upon layer of truth. It is shocking, uncomfortable, and real for the reader. These writers elevate the act from one of communication to an art form. They are my inspiration.

For me, writing's fundamental lesson is that it is not about pleasing people. It is an expression of my own truth presented in my own way. There will be people who dislike both what I have to say and the words I use to say it. They will question my perspective as someone in a race or class or religion or gender different from their own. At the beginning, I was afraid of the judgment of others, in particular those who would vilify me. I wanted to keep it small and play it safe. But if my goal is to create art, then I cannot also apologize for it. I can only put it out into the world and see what happens to it and because of it. This lesson's corollary is that you know you are being true to yourself if you no longer care what others think about the art you are creating. Through writing I have learned an essential axiom for living.

When I am stuck in a writing quagmire, I feel frustrated and annoyed. I know something is missing, but I don't know what. Or, the words sound like I plunked them down with a heavy hand—they are awkward and officious. Am I being too instructive? I ask myself. Do I sound like a snob? At these times I lose all my writing confidence. The cobra bares its fangs. I breathe. I walk away from the desk and look for inspiration. I rifle through my writing journal, where I keep all my treasures: the words of the fearless, the craft of the masters. Reading a couple of favorite poems usually does the trick. Writing is art-making, and art-making is not easy. Being vulnerable is a powerful act, but getting to that place can be excruciating.

Doing the work of writing is easy, but holding one's center is painfully difficult. I lie in Pigeon and try to keep my mind at bay, to let myself sense the discomfort in my hips without panicking or pulling up. Like writing, this is an act of letting go. Writing from your heart, speaking your truth, and saying the things you need to say is where the real work starts. The muse inside each of us, disguised as a lowly pigeon, asks us to offer up our authentic selves and surrender to our power to create.

ON VULNERABILITY
CORPSE POSE, SAVASANA

In this final relaxation pose in your practice, lie on your back in a comfortable position, supporting your knees if you need to or draping a blanket across your body. Lie completely still, with your arms extended to the sides and your palms facing up. Feel yourself melt into the mat and into the floor beneath you. Allow yourself to be heavy. Allow your body to breathe and let your thoughts fade into the background. Your sinews and muscles are rushing to make sense of what you have just put your body through. Receive the wisdom of your practice.

I woke up in the hospital on the day after my surgery—the day after the Boston Marathon bombings—and saw the dawn easing over the Zakim bridge, all soft and blousy, pink and lavender. I thought of those many others also waking to face this new day, some without limbs or flesh, so many in pain, none of whom had planned, as I had, to be here. It was unfair, wrong, heartless for them to be watching this same dawn from these same windows. I wanted to be gone as soon as possible, to shake the feeling of the capriciousness of fate, to stand on solid ground. I wanted all those others to be whole again, for time to go backwards, for the dawn to be yesterday's innocent blush.

I sat up. This took effort, as my abdomen was sore and my muscles felt weak and disconnected. I was tired of being in corpse pose, though, prone on the bed, uncomfortable and restless. The room was quiet and the noises of the hospital seemed to be holding their breath. I faced the dawn and asked for all of us to be as we were, even as I knew we all must now be as we are.

Finding out I had to have colon surgery was a blow to my idea of how my carefully crafted life would proceed. In the span of six weeks, I went from perfect health to a hospital gurney in the heart of Big Medicine. The surgery was a success and I am physically whole, but I am not the same me. We cannot be the same after close calls or what feel like close calls. We are humbled and we are strengthened, all at once. I am not going to escape health worries because I cannot control them. I am not special or somehow exempt. Things that happen to "other people" are frightening when they happen to us.

Being vulnerable is transformative—in fact far more powerful than my typical instinct to build a wall and go private. I reached out this time to family and friends, told them I was afraid, and asked them to keep me in their thoughts. Through the love and grace they returned to me, I understood that admitting I was not unbreakable made me more human. I learned that my flaws or imperfections are what make me unique, and in having them I am not unique. The trials we endure leave us changed, and the desire to be back to being the same is a lost opportunity to grow.

I left the hospital under the watch of armed guards, wearing my yoga pants like a security blanket, carrying my lovely flowers. It felt strange to be vertical and surreal to be in a city under attack. We drove past the Charles River and saw the sailboats dipping and twirling, the cyclists flying down the path, the runners and walkers and strollers zooming across the bridges. Life was moving on, lives were being put back together, joy was in the offing. Even after tearing everything beautiful apart, we were knitting ourselves back together to what felt right and whole. This was a city's Savasana and one for me: time to recognize both gratitude and strength and push on.

In the first few months of yoga classes I would regularly fall asleep during Savasana. I awakened a few times at the end of class to discover with embarrassment that I had been snoring. I then challenged myself to stay awake through the few minutes of this active meditation by checking in with my limbs at regular intervals. It helped, but was not very restful. That trick evolved into focusing on my breath and staying present, also an effort but surprisingly energizing. Now during Savasana I am so awake that my thoughts drift shamelessly and most often to writing. I take heart that I am at least exploring the mind-body connection while supposedly meditating. Occasionally, I have a tremendous insight during Savasana and I fret that I will not remember it; it takes unfamiliar discipline to trust that these personal revelations will come back to me when they are most needed.

I have wondered often over these three years of yoga what that Chinese symbol was that appeared in my very first Savasana. At times my curiosity has gotten the better of me and I have spent hours searching for it online, in vain. Finally, a friend of a friend, who is Chinese, was able to properly decipher it. I drew it out as best I could, although my recollection was hazy. I learned it is not a real Chinese character, as such symbols are quite exact in their brushstrokes, and each component is essential to the whole. It is most reminiscent, though, of the symbol for Beauty.

Beauty.

Its meaning for me is profound. I have found beauty in yoga, beauty in writing, beauty in my struggles both on and off the mat, and beauty in coming more fully into myself. What makes beauty is the component parts being brought together in just the right way, whatever that is right now, at this moment, in this place.

We can grow all our lives. We must leave the child's pose behind and face what makes us afraid. For me, this was a deep desire to write, to marry words in service of truth. I have had to take up arms and stand my ground and tame serpents to get myself to this place. I have had to lay down arms and shape shift and sit with grief and find balance in my life. I have had to build bridges across chasms that seem impossibly wide. I have had to remember that with love there are no limits. I have had to be vulnerable when I have wanted to be fully armored. I have had to quiet my ego and listen to my heart. I have had to allow the practice—of writing, of yoga—to change me so that it is a new version of me completing the work I started.

Whether we are conscious of it or not, we are weaving our new selves each day: layers of learning and trial, little knots of frustration, silken yarns for joy, tears in the fabric that have become part of the design. I am the intricate tapestry of my physical being and my mental abilities, my emotional girding and my spiritual insight. I keep on weaving, casting out the shuttle across the loom of time, shifting the warp when I gain a little wisdom, casting back again. It is the most I, or anyone, can do in this exquisite life. It is as simple as breathing, and, like the victorious breath of the yogini, as full of mystery and promise.

Bring yourself back to awareness. Move your fingers and toes gently and ease your mind back to the room. Bend your knees toward your chest and roll over onto your right side for a moment. Then, with your eyes closed and your head heavy, bring yourself up to a comfortable seated position. Breathe deeply, one final cleansing breath. With your palms together in front of your heart, bow to your teacher and to yourself, for they are the same.

ACKNOWLEDGEMENTS

First, I must acknowledge you, my reader. Thank you for reading my words and making them your own. As yoginis say, the divine in me honors the divine in you.

I acknowledge with love my mother, Judith M. Carey, who gave me the gift of writing through her life and in her spirit. I know she would be proud that I have put my words into the world.

I thank my first yoga instructor, Taylor McHugh, who held the space for me in those early months to explore body, mind and heart alone on my mat. Many, many thanks to my long-time yoga instructor, Janine Agoglia, who shares her gifts with humor, grace and wisdom, and who reminds us to be kind to ourselves, always.

Tremendous thanks go to my early readers, Carolyn Heilman, Carl Scholz, Janine Agoglia, Freya Pendleton, Kerry Stratton, Dana Scholz, and Jennifer Flaxman, whose insights gave shape and sense to this book. Thanks also to Freya and Laird, and Karla and

Dave, who hosted the first and second Mandala Writers Circle retreats in their lovely mountain homes; it was there that I first battled the cobra and began the journey to complete this book.

Many thanks to my extraordinary illustrator and father-in-law, Arthur Scholz, for his talent and generosity in making this book shine.

Words seem insufficient for the thanks I owe to Carolyn, my dear friend and writing partner, co-founder of the Mandala Writers Circle, fellow seeker. Your listening heart shaped this book, and your encouragement inspired me to keep plugging away at it. You are a gifted artist and treasured friend.

My two daughters, Claudia and Dana, make me grateful every day that I am their mother. You are beautiful and creative and wise, both luminous warriors. I am so proud and excited to watch each of you pursue your dreams.

My husband Carl is my biggest champion. He has been asking me to write this book, any book, since we were teenagers. Thank you for believing in me and for loving me every day as I wound my wayward path. I love you beyond words.

ABOUT THE AUTHOR

Leah Carey is a writer, entrepreneur, and executive coach. She has worked in the corporate world for over 25 years, both as an internal consultant and as an independent consultant to high-technology firms. Leah is a dedicated reader and yoga practitioner. She is the mother of two grown daughters and lives with her husband in the suburbs of Boston. *As Simple As Breathing: On Yoga, Writing, and Life* is her first book.

More of Leah's thoughts on books and writing can be found at her website, The Mandala Writers Circle, www.mandalawriterscircle.com.

www.ingramcontent.com/pod-product-compliance
Lightning Source LLC
Chambersburg PA
CBHW022118040426
42450CB00006B/753